Migration, Minorities and Citizenship

General Editors: **Zig Layton-Henry**, Professor of Politics, University of Warwick; and **Danièle Joly**, Professor, Director, Centre for Research in Ethnic Relations, University of Warwick

Titles include:

Muhammad Anwar, Patrick Roach and Ranjit Sondhi (*editors*)
FROM LEGISLATION TO INTEGRATION?
Race Relations in Britain

James A. Beckford, Danièle Joly and Farhad Khosrokhavar
MUSLIMS IN PRISON
Challenge and Change in Britain and France

Christophe Bertossi (*editor*)
EUROPEAN ANTI-DISCRIMINATION AND THE POLITICS OF CITIZENSHIP
Britain and France

Thomas Faist and Andreas Ette (*editors*)
THE EUROPEANIZATION OF NATIONAL POLICIES AND POLITICS OF IMMIGRATION
Between Autonomy and the European Union

Thomas Faist and Peter Kivisto (*editors*)
DUAL CITIZENSHIP IN GLOBAL PERSPECTIVE
From Unitary to Multiple Citizenship

Adrian Favell
PHILOSOPHIES OF INTEGRATION
Immigration and the Idea of Citizenship in France and Britain

Agata Górny and Paulo Ruspini (*editors*)
MIGRATION IN THE NEW EUROPE
East-West Revisited

James Hampshire
CITIZENSHIP AND BELONGING
Immigration and the Politics of Democratic Governance in Postwar Britain

John R. Hinnells (*editor*)
RELIGIOUS RECONSTRUCTION IN THE SOUTH ASIAN DIASPORAS
From One Generation to Another

Danièle Joly
GLOBAL CHANGES IN ASYLUM REGIMES (*editor*)
Closing Doors

Zig Layton-Henry and Czarina Wilpert (*editors*)
CHALLENGING RACISM IN BRITAIN AND GERMANY

Jørgen S. Nielsen
TOWARDS A EUROPEAN ISLAM

Pontus Odmalm
MIGRATION POLICIES AND POLITICAL PARTICIPATION
Inclusion or Intrusion in Western Europe

Aspasia Papadopoulou-Kourkoula
TRANSIT MIGRATION
The Missing Link Between Emigration and Settlement

Jan Rath (*editor*)
IMMIGRANT BUSINESSES
The Economic, Political and Social Environment

Carl-Ulrik Schierup (*editor*)
SCRAMBLE FOR THE BALKANS
Nationalism, Globalism and the Political Economy of Reconstruction

Maarten Vink
LIMITS OF EUROPEAN CITIZENSHIP
European Integration and Domestic Immigration Policies

Östen Wahlbeck
KURDISH DIASPORAS
A Comparative Study of Kurdish Refugee Communities

Migration, Minorities and Citizenship
Series Standing Order ISBN 978-0-333-71047-0 (hardback) and 978-0-333-80338-7
(paperback)
(*outside North America only*)

You can receive future titles in this series as they are published by placing a standing order.
Please contact your bookseller or, in case of difficulty, write to us at the address below with
your name and address, the title of the series and the ISBN quoted above.

Customer Services Department, Macmillan Distribution Ltd, Houndmills, Basingstoke,
Hampshire RG21 6XS, England.

Transit Migration

The Missing Link between Emigration and Settlement

Aspasia Papadopoulou-Kourkoula

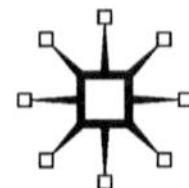

First published 2008 by
PALGRAVE MACMILLAN
Houndmills, Basingstoke, Hampshire RG21 6XS and
175 Fifth Avenue, New York, N.Y. 10010
Companies and representatives throughout the world

PALGRAVE MACMILLAN is the global academic imprint of the Palgrave Macmillan division of St. Martin's Press, LLC and of Palgrave Macmillan Ltd. Macmillan® is a registered trademark in the United States, United Kingdom and other countries. Palgrave is a registered trademark in the European Union and other countries.

ISBN-13: 978–0–230–55533–4   hardback
ISBN-10: 0–230–55533–0   hardback

This book is printed on paper suitable for recycling and made from fully managed and sustained forest sources. Logging, pulping and manufacturing processes are expected to conform to the environmental regulations of the country of origin.

A catalogue record for this book is available from the British Library.

Library of Congress Cataloging-in-Publication Data

Papadopoulou-Kourkoula, Aspasia, 1976–
   Transit migration : the missing link between emigration and
   settlement / Aspasia Papadopoulou-Kourkoula.
      p. cm.
   Includes bibliographical references and index.
   ISBN 978–0–230–55533–4 (alk. paper)
    1. Emigration and immigration–Social aspects. 2. Immigrants–Social
   conditions. 3. Europe–Emigration and immigration–Social aspects.
   4. Immigrants–Europe–Social conditions. I. Title.
   JV6225.P37 2008
   304.8–dc22
                                                         2008020653

10   9   8   7   6   5   4   3   2   1
17   16   15   14   13   12   11   10   09   08

Printed and bound in Great Britain by
CPI Antony Rowe, Chippenham and Eastbourne

To Constantin

Contents

Preface

Scene 1: Penteli refugee camp, Athens, winter 2002
We are sitting together with Nermin in her room and she is telling me about the job she used to have, a teacher in a primary school in Suleimaniya. Sipping the tea she made for me, I hear about how much she likes teaching and children. She wants to work again, she has missed it. She also wants to have children she says, it's been two years since they got married but with all this moving around and the constant uncertainty it was just not possible. They arrived here about one year ago and they have been living in this room ever since. The room looks as if they arrived yesterday. Clothes piled up on a chair, a few belongings here and there and that's all. I am asking whether they are leaving soon. Who knows, she says, it depends, in the end they may stay in Greece as well. 'We just want to have a normal life soon, just like you have', she says as she sees me to the door.

Scene 2: UNHCR Rabat Office, Morocco, spring 2006
The taxi drops me off at the UNHCR office. A crowd of over 30 people, all Africans, is gathered at the gate and there seems to be a furore. Some are waving a note they hold in their hands, they have come for the interview. A woman is holding her baby in front of her and argues with someone. She needs to take the baby to the doctor she says, and she cannot afford it. A young man, clutching his mobile in one hand, seems to have a leading role, he is discussing with the guards, while four or five others are standing in a circle around him. Some others are waiting further back, gathered under a tree. They have come to register. The guard is calling the name of someone that has an interview, but nobody seems to respond. As I approach the gate, I hear someone saying that this person has left. For Spain, he explains. Last time they saw him was two weeks ago. No news since.

This book was written in two phases. The first phase was in the years 2000–4, when I was reading for a PhD degree at Oxford University. I picked the case of Kurdish asylum seekers in Greece to research and embarked on a search to explain how reception policies affect the course of refugee movements. After a couple of interviews and visits, I realized that the reasons that affected the course of movement of the

Kurds were much more diverse, complex and ambiguous than just the outcome of reception policies in the country. In addition, the course of movement was neither predictable nor was it corresponding to plans they had made in the past. In fact, most of the people I spoke to were living in Greece in a condition that was in-between, for prolonged periods of time. Some were even undocumented for years. This population was invisible; some would eventually appear as statistics on asylum applications in Greece, or in another country, or even as a file in a future regularization programme. In the process of writing, the analysis of the transit stage and its relation to irregularity and asylum took shape and evolved.

The second phase of the book was written a couple of years later, after I took a break and switched sides, going from research to policy analysis and project management. Working with the Global Commission on International Migration in Geneva helped me see things in perspective, from the local to the global, and from the migrants' point of view to that of policy makers. I had the chance to work with UNHCR and run a project of capacity building for asylum in five North African countries in 2005. The project struck at the heart of the issue of migrants and refugees in transit, and made it all the more clear to me how the phenomenon was not limited to a particular country or region. There were many similarities between the situation in North Africa and that observed during my fieldwork in Greece. I also found it striking how little transit migration was debated in policy circles, despite its growing scale and multi-level impact on states and people. Living and working in the region was an eye-opener in many ways, and added a further perspective to my understanding of the phenomenon, namely the views and capacities of non-European countries in the migration debate. The material and observations on North Africa presented in this book were collected during these two years of stay in Tunisia and Morocco (2005–6). However, the views presented in this book remain my own, and do not necessarily represent those of the UNHCR.

I am grateful to the institutions and a number of individuals who have supported me, each in their own way. I am grateful to all the migrants I interviewed for sharing their memories, experiences and anxieties with me, to the UNHCR office in Athens for giving me access to archives, and the social workers in the refugee camps and staff at NGOs for their time and precious information. I am equally indebted to all the other scholars upon whose work I have drawn. My primary debt is owed to my supervisors at Oxford University, Ali Rogers and Erik Swyngedouw, for their intellectual guidance, constant support and comments in the course of research. This book grew out of the uniquely invigorating environment of Oxford University and St.Antony's College and I am grateful for having had the chance to be there. I would also like to thank the people at the 'Cosmopolis' group at the Department of Geography, Vrije Universiteit Brussel in Belgium for hosting me during the last months of writing the thesis. I am very grateful to Effie Voutira for her comments on the PhD draft, and Renée Hirschon for our discussions that have always been a source of inspiration. A special debt of gratitude to the Economic and Social Research Council in the United Kingdom and the Greek State Scholarships Board (IKY) for financing my postgraduate studies and making this possible. I would also like to thank the people at the GCIM, especially Asa Carlander, and Khalid Koser for his encouragement and support. I owe a lot to Jeff Crisp for his guidance in drafting policy analysis and for being an example of balanced, comprehensive and concise writing. Thank you also to the people at the UNHCR in Tunisia, Morocco and in Geneva, Ruven Menikdiwela, and particularly Johannes van der Klaauw for being a source of inspiration. I am grateful to Laurence Hart for sharing his views with me and for constructive comments. Last but not least, I would like to thank my editor, Philippa Grand, for her confidence and support.

Finally, the biggest thank you goes to my husband, Constantin, for his encouragement, constant inspiration and support, for being there to raise my spirits when they were low and for reading and editing the draft. I could not have written this book without him.

Disclaimer

The views expressed in this book are solely those of the author and do not necessarily represent the views of the European Commission, of the United Nations High Commissioner for Refugees, or of any other institution or body.

List of Abbreviations

ACP	Africa, the Caribbean and Pacific Group of States
ANSA	Agenzia Nazionale Stampa Associata
APDH	Asociación pro Derechos Humanos de Andalucía
BAD	Banque Africaine de Development/African Development Bank
CEAS	Common European Asylum System
CIS	Commonwealth of Independent States
DCI	Development Cooperation Instrument
DRC	Democratic Republic of Congo
EC	European Commission
ECRE	European Council on Refugees and Exiles
EESC	European Economic and Social Committee
ENP	European Neighbourhood Policy
ENPI	European Neighbourhood Policy Instrument
ERF	European Refugee Fund
ERNK	Eniya Rizgariya Netewa Kurdistan/Kurdish National Liberation Front
FRONTEX	European Agency for the Management of Operational Cooperation at the External Borders of the Member States of the European Union
HLWG	High Level Working Group on Migration and Asylum
ICMPD	International Centre for Migration Policy Development
ICRC	International Committee of the Red Cross
IDPs	Internally displaced persons
ILO	International Labour Organization
IMO	International Maritime Organization
IOM	International Organization for Migration
JHA	Justice and Home Affairs
LIBE	Committee on Civil Liberties, Justice and Home Affairs (European Parliament)
MARRI	Migration, Asylum and Refugees Regional Initiative
MIREM	Return Migration to the Maghreb
MPI	Migration Policy Institute
MPO	Ministry of Public Order
OAU	Organization of African Union/African Unity
OSCE	Organization for Security and Cooperation in Europe

PCA	Partnership Cooperation Agreement
PKK	Partiya Karkerên Kurdistan/Kurdistan Workers Party
RSD	Refugee Status Determination
SAR	Search and Rescue
SEECP	South East European Cooperation Process
SIVE	Sistema Integrado de Vigilancia Exterior
SOLAS	International Convention for the Safety of Life at Sea
TACIS	Technical Aid to the Commonwealth of Independent States
TPC	Transit Processing Centres
UAE	United Arab Emirates
UNECE	United Nations Economic Commission for Europe
UNHCR	United Nations High Commissioner for Refugees
UNODC	United Nations Office on Drugs and Crime

1
Introduction

> ... It's been two years since we got here ... When we first arrived
> with my husband, we didn't know what to do; should we stay?
> There was no hope to get asylum. Should we go? He had friends in
> France and they were telling us to go there and from there we
> could go to England; but we had just arrived in Greece, I was so
> tired and we were running out of money. We said OK let's wait a
> bit and see, when we have money perhaps we will try to go. We
> stayed in Lavrio [refugee camp] for six months and slowly, slowly
> my husband found a job here, a job there, so we managed; I didn't
> work. We moved to a flat together with five others. We were saving
> money and sending half to my mother and sister at home ... In the
> beginning it was really difficult, I was crying a lot, but we didn't
> tell them how hard it was in Greece. We put on our best clothes,
> went to the Acropolis and took a photo, and sent it to them. They
> thought that we made it, and that we are happy ... And it's been
> two years now.
>
> (Interview with Kurd, Athens, November 2001)

Irregular migration makes headlines in Europe. Whether in the style of
heart-bleeding compassion or misleading security concerns, it certainly
creates some hype. Then, migrants 'disappear' for some time, to surface
again in public debates as an asylum, regularization or integration
issue. There is the time spent in-between which somehow goes un-
noticed. This book is about this obscure phase and the way in which it
ties in and effects the whole migration process.

In modern history, the number of people on the move around the
world has never been greater. Both the number of regular and irregular
migrants and the number of refugees appear to be on the rise. While

Europe is one of the major destinations, the relatively limited possibilities for legal entry mean that thousands of migrants risk their lives crossing borders and seas illegally. At the same time as many survive the perilous journey, a staggering number perishes. The Red Cross estimates that 2000 migrants drown every year in the Mediterranean trying to reach Europe.

European states are struggling to find a way to manage migration and prevent human tragedies. Yet so far the measures seem to deliver only short-term results. Part of the problem is that migration is typically addressed as a local crisis and not as a broader process. The realization that the issue begs for regional perspectives, regional approaches and common efforts has only started to make its way to policy circles.

Migration is usually approached through traditional 'static' dichotomies ('emigration/immigration', 'forced/voluntary', 'regular/irregular', 'sending/receiving countries'). The reality of migration movements is, however, far more complex and cannot be grasped by such a dualistic approach. Migration is a process with multiple variables in terms of place, time, means and motivation. The same migrant may – and very often does – combine legal and illegal means and make various attempts through different channels before reaching a final destination. This destination may or may not become the *final* destination depending on various factors and circumstances in a person's life.

The unlawful nature of irregular migration makes it impossible to maintain accurate data as to the number of irregular migrants. Yet, it is estimated that for every one person caught entering the EU illegally, two to four others pass unhindered (Salt, 2002). There are also many ways in which one can become an irregular migrant. They include: entry without documents; entry with fake documents; legal entry but illegal stay/work (e.g. with a tourist visa that has expired); legal entry and stay but illegal work (informal); legal stay and work that gradually becomes illegal (work and residence permit expired or impossible to renew); legal stay while awaiting the outcome of an asylum application, but irregular stay after the application has been rejected.

A common characteristic in the above scenarios is that they depend on the coming about of a particular opportunity – a tourist visa, a gap in border control, a work permit, refugee status. In waiting for these opportunities to arise, more and more migrants and refugees stay in peripheral countries 'in transit', sometimes for very long periods of time. Some find themselves stuck, unable to go on or to go back home.

1.1 Transit

No standard definition of transit migration exists today.[1] Major organizations and policy groups such as the IOM, the ICMPD, the UNECE or the Council of Europe have often included transit migration in their agenda, yet there is no commonly accepted definition. Information on transit migration is based mostly on empirical case studies that have also provided descriptions of the phenomenon. Many of these studies were conducted in the mid-1990s (namely the studies commissioned by the IOM, in Eastern Europe and the former Soviet Union, in Turkey, etc.) and then again in recent years, since 2003. These early studies, at a time when nobody in Europe was talking about transit migration, are evidence of the fact that the phenomenon was already happening in the East. Comparing the old with the more recent studies, a common trait emerges in that they all highlight the importance of migrant *intentions* in transit and the plan to migrate further to another host country.

UNECE was among the first to talk about transit migration in 1993, which they described as 'migration in one country *with the intention of seeking the possibility* there to emigrate to another country as the country of final destination' (UNECE, 1993, p. 7). What is interesting in this description is that the continuation of the journey is contingent upon opportunities available en route.

İçduygu conducted research in Turkey and defined transit as 'migrants [who] come to a country of destination *with the intention* of going and staying in another country' (İçduygu, 1995, p.127, emphasis added). In his consequent work (2000, 2003, 2005), İçduygu emphasized these intentions and placed the analysis of transit migration in the context of globalization and the relations between centre and periphery. Similarly, a conference organized by the Council of Europe on transit migration in 2004 describes a transit migrant as 'a foreign national in a legal or irregular situation whose *intention* is to leave his or her current country of residence "as soon as possible" in order to reach a third country' (CoE, 2004, p. 121, emphasis added).

Ivakhniouk (2004) took the analysis one step further, to aspects such as the lack of protection and uncertainty – for example, by prolonging a transit stay because it is impossible to move further, or leaving after unsuccessful stay in a destination country. Ivakhniouk summarized these as the human dimension, the economic dimension (irregular employment), the security dimension and entanglement of migration and smuggling with criminal groups, and the social dimension of transit migration.

A Danish publication on Mediterranean Transit Migration in 2006 provided a similar definition. Sorensen (2006) in that volume explains transit migration as a consequence of geography and the regions' proximity to the prosperous European Union. Cassarino and Fargues (2006) add that transit may differ between countries according to the policy framework, social and cultural affinity, the role of migrant networks and so on.

Düvell's (2006) work is both the most recent and more detailed theoretical discussion of the concept. He identifies a number of misconceptions and argues that transit migration is a blurred and politicized concept. Düvell complements the analysis with two further parameters in determining the course of movement, the role of restrictive policies and that of class.

All these studies have contributed substantially to our understanding of transit migration to date. Nevertheless, none seems to have struck a balance between the various reasons that might make migrants transit. Some tend to overemphasize the role of migrant intentions and strategies; others tend to reduce the whole issue to geography, or to the impact of 'Fortress Europe'. But most importantly, they approach transit migration as yet another dichotomy: transit/ non-transit. What is missing is an integrated approach that links the transit phase to the broader migration process.

In this book transit migration is understood as the situation between emigration and settlement that is characterized by indefinite migrant stay, legal or illegal, and may or may not develop into further migration depending on a series of structural and individual factors.[2] Although intentions are an important factor that shapes individual migration strategies, they are not singled out in this definition because they are part of a much more complex equation. Macro-level structures – such as policies, social networks – and micro-level factors discussed in this book prove to be at least as important. Furthermore, intentions are neither formed independently of the context in which they arise, nor are they fixed. They evolve and adapt to the realities that transit migrants will encounter on the way. In fact, intentions are very often much more vague than one might expect. The migrant very often does not have a clear or precise idea of where he would like to migrate to.

A second remark is that in this definition settlement is characterized as *indefinite* not only because we, the observers, have no way of knowing the duration of the stay, but more importantly because the migrants themselves cannot know that duration. Reality will often develop very differently from the plans a migrant might have had. A short stopover in a given country may eventually translate into a five-year stay. What was planned as a final 'settlement' destination may turn out to be only one step in a much larger journey. Similarly, a destination that was planned as merely a necessary point in passage may eventually become a place of permanent settlement. It is not only the duration of stay that is unknown, but also whether a particular stage in the migration process will turn out to be temporary or not. In that sense, the definition of transit migration as a situation that '*may or may not develop into further migration*' is not simply a truism, but a translation of the inherent ambivalence of transit migration. It is only *a posteriori* that the observer (and the migrant) knows if a particular stay was temporary or not.

This approach challenges the traditional linear view of migration as a clearly structured process, characterized by distinct phases such as *departure, journey, arrival, integration*. The route and duration of the journey can only be tentative at best. Whether a particular phase in the migration route is part of the journey or it is part of the arrival is an open question that can only be answered a posteriori. And because of those ambiguities, integration is an issue that may pose itself every step of the way. While from an academic perspective all this may make for a more complex definition, from the migrants' perspective the uncertainty is yet another source of insecurity.

Transit migration is not a migrant category and not a new policy area – it is a process and a contingency. Transit migration is a phase that cuts across various migrant categories: irregular migrants, asylum seekers, refugees granted asylum, regularized migrants, students, trafficked persons may all find themselves in the condition of transit at some point. In North Africa and Eastern Europe, shifting between categories is common. As the following chapters will illustrate, some migrants come with a plan and, indeed, the intention to re-emigrate as quickly as possible; others, however, may not have a plan and will migrate randomly, trying to find possibilities – of stay or further emigration – in the next receiving country. Everything is possible.

It should be underlined that the term 'transit migrants' is used in this book to refer to both economic migrants and refugees found in mixed flows, or what is known as the 'asylum-migration nexus'. While asylum and irregular migration are different issues and concern different policy areas, they do overlap in three circumstances: when a rejected asylum seeker becomes an irregular migrant, when an irregular migrant uses the asylum system as a means of migration, and in the transit flows when both refugees and economic migrants use the same route and irregular path.

Transit migration is not new. There were always transit routes, transit migrants and transit cities. Yet, the scale of the phenomenon makes it a whole new situation today: migrants arrive and stay in certain countries *en masse*, trying to reach the next EU member state. A number of countries in the periphery of the European Union have turned into transit countries par excellence – and this is indeed something new. The landscape and geography of transit/receiving countries is constantly changing – the transit countries of today are the destination countries of tomorrow. The fact that transit migration has become a popular new topic is only a consequence of these new developments.

Transit migration is not a uniform type of experience either. It is also not linear, but may involve numerous stops and movements in rather unexpected directions. The next chapters present routes, some of which may not 'make sense' in the standard origin/destination rationale. The transit phase also involves diverse experiences. In some countries, transit migration is very closely related to trafficking; in other cases registering for studies is a common transit migration strategy.

Some argue that transit migration essentially is a code word for 'irregular migration' (Düvell, 2006) and indeed some scholars often use the terms interchangeably in their analysis. However, while the two may overlap, they are not synonymous. A person holding a residence permit, or registered as an asylum seeker or as a student may also be 'in transit'. The confusion may come from the fact that transit migration is mostly mentioned and discussed when it overlaps with irregular migration.

What creates transit migration in a particular country? Geography is most commonly cited as the obvious reason. The restrictive character of EU migration and asylum policy and the absence of legal migration channels are major factors creating a pool of transit migrants in the periphery of Europe; nevertheless, this explanation often seems limited, and is dominated by a rhetoric of 'EU externalization' that is too polarized to account for all factors shaping transit migration. In this book I will try to show that transit migration can be a result of a large number of factors. These include: socioeconomic development and change in the region; efficiency of border controls; settlement and employment prospects for migrants; asylum policy and reception infrastructure; migration policy and ability to obtain residence permits; ability to integrate, to speak the local language, and their relation to the host society; resources available to finance the next leg of the trip;

social and smuggling networks to assist in the organization of the journey; family ties in a particular country that make it the desired destination; personal ambitions, determination or fear; the sense of honour and social pressures from home to accomplish the migration venture.

Another question that should be answered is about what sets the limit between the moment when the transit phase ends and becomes settlement. Duration alone cannot be the defining factor. Instead, it is the degree to which a migrant engages with the structures and opportunities in the receiving countries and invests in hopes, money, contacts and infrastructure in order to settle properly.

Beyond specialized research, transit migration is seldom developed in policy debates. Any mention is usually limited to the acknowledgement that certain countries have turned into transit countries as they host large numbers of migrants waiting to go to Europe. In fact, the emphasis is usually placed on the latter: on the direct effect that this has on European countries. The actual situation of transit migration and its consequences for the migrants, the countries in question, and the indirect effects on European countries seem to be missing from the debate. In this book I will argue that the transit condition may be a crucial link in the analysis of international migration, as it can determine the course of future receiving countries, migrant communities and return possibilities.

A number of reasons can be advanced as to why transit is not debated. First, by its very nature, transit migration is not quantifiable and what is more, it overlaps with many migrant categories. Second, public perceptions are governed by a misconception that all one has to do is wait: transit migrants will eventually leave for another country. Yet, as this book shows, most transit migrants stay for long periods of time and many eventually settle in the transit country. Third, transit migrants are not seen as a target group by policy makers because it is assumed they do not participate in the host society in which they are presently staying; whereas, in fact, they work, spend, consume, learn the language and have medical and education needs. Fourth, another common bias is that transit migration only happens in certain parts of the world; in fact it happens everywhere, and with higher concentration in regions close to a popular destination. In particular it is commonly thought that transit migration only happens in low-income or developing countries; but the chapter on Greece shows that transit migration also happens inside Europe. Sangatte was also a case of transit migration in Europe (CoE, 2004). Finally, transit migration is overlooked because transit countries are usually reluctant to accept the reality of migration and fear that if they develop policy measures, migrants will eventually settle. In other words, the false impression that all transit migrants are bound to leave sooner or later causes transit migration to be used as a pretext for the lack of will to develop a migration policy.

1.2   Focus and methodological considerations

This book is about the experience of transit migration outside and inside European borders and its impact on states and people. I will argue that transit migration is a complex process that puts pressure on countries and neighbours, and more importantly, renders migrants and refugees particularly vulnerable. Some of the questions to be addressed are: Why do migrants stay 'in transit' and how do they experience this situation? What sustains transit migration? What policy challenges do transit and destination countries face?

I use three examples from the fringes of Europe to analyse transit migration; Greece, the North African countries, and Eastern Europe and CIS. North Africa and Eastern Europe are known transit areas that have attracted substantial attention in recent years. Greece has not been in the spotlight, definitely not as much as Spain and Italy, even though the scale of irregular and transit migration is as high or even higher. All three examples demonstrate that the phenomenon is not limited to a particular country or area: aside from certain local features, it is globally identical in Europe's eastern and southern borders, as well as on the inside and outside of European borders. On the migrants' side, the case of Kurds in Greece is used as a typical example of the transit experience.[3]

This book doesn't take sides; it is as much about the migrants, their feelings, plans and trajectories, as it is about state and EU policies. The book aims to present both sides, top-down and bottom-up, and what is more, it aims to present how these two interact. From the countries' perspective, I examine national policies and strategies for cooperation at the regional or bilateral level, emphasizing in particular the EU factor. It is striking that in all three cases examined, state policies are weak and inefficient. From the migrants' perspective, I will analyse decision-making and how transit is actually experienced. The journey and crossing of borders is part and parcel of this transit stage, and is illustrated through examples of routes and smuggling practices in most of the countries in question. Family ties and social networks, local and transnational, are instrumental in shaping migration strategies. Social ties with the host society are of equal importance at the transit as they are at the integration phase. They play the role of 'support structures', providing resources and assistance for reception and survival in the transit country. Backed by these support structures, migrants carve out a space for mobilization and negotiation. This was the case in Greece through the informal social networks developed with the locals and with activists (Chapter 3), and it also happens in Morocco with local and European activist groups (Chapter 5).

The book is based on background research on the selected regions during the last three years and fieldwork in Greece during the period 2001–3, comprising in-depth interviews with 50 Kurds in Athens, semi-structured interviews with 20 policy makers, and discourse analysis.[4] In addition, research in North Africa was supported through my first-hand experience of being resident and working in the region with one of the main actors in the field, UNHCR, in the year 2005.

Two-thirds of the interviews were conducted with asylum seekers living in the refugee camps of Lavrio and Penteli on the outskirts of Athens, and the Reception Hall 'Nafsika' in the city centre. Some were newcomers, while others had been there for some time, even for a few years. They were not certain about staying in Greece. The rest of the Kurds had been 'settled' in the city for a few years and did not seem to consider migrating again.

I have used narratives as a source and as a 'voice' in this book in order to illustrate the experience through the eyes of the people in question. The story of Bêrîcan and Sîwan, presented in Chapters 3 and 4, and various interview quotes give us the possibility to understand individual practices and social relations behind these.[5]

While studying this topic, I was faced with a number of methodological questions that affected the conclusions drawn in this book. They all revolve around the central question of how one can study transit migration. Are people in transit just because they say that they want to move on? And linked to this, how can transit migration be verified, if only retrospectively? Is it possible to identify migrants while they are 'being in transit' since it is impossible to know the outcome of this process? Most studies are conducted with asylum seekers in receiving countries, identifying retrospectively that they had transited through various countries. Or they are conducted in known transit regions where it is assumed that most migrants – and particularly asylum seekers – are in transit, even if one cannot be certain whether they will actually leave. I interviewed both cases; migrants who seemed to be 'in transit' and others who seemed to be 'settled'. In both cases the transit condition was not identified in terms of time, but in terms of the characteristics that define the transit experience.

Düvell (2006) argues that one should distinguish between 'mental' and 'actual' transit migration, and that intentions are the determining factor. Transit migration is a state of mind, he argues. In the next chapters I will show that intentions or plans are not always the crucial factor. There is a state of mind of being in-between places and life stages, in limbo. But there is also a very tangible side to it in terms of living conditions, access to protection, rights and opportunities in the host country that makes transit migration not only a mental but also an actual condition.

Are narratives to be trusted as truth? What if people make things up when talking to the researcher? In her discussion of validity in research, Hammersley (1992) proposes to examine whether claims made are credible and plausible. In other words, accounts cannot be tested for actually being true/false, but for having or not having a rational basis. In addition, it is not only the *what* but also the *why* information is selected to be presented, and to *whom*. The fact that Kurds had been attributed a stereotypical political label in Greece (see Chapter 4) also affected migrant self-presentation, through a constant effort from their side to meet my 'demand characteristics' (Plummer, 2001) and say things that they thought I would want to hear, and a constant effort from my side to read between the lines. A Kurdish woman gave a very good description of trust, and of how and why information is presented:

> Look, there are some things that I am not going to tell you, you will understand why, I can't tell you. But what I am going to say is true, and whether you believe me or not, that's up to you. But it is true. And I am telling you those things because someone has to talk about them, and someone has to write and people should know about them ... And I like you, that's why I am telling you these things, otherwise I wouldn't say a word to you; or I would tell you ... whatever.
>
> (Kurd, interview in Athens, January 2002)

1.3   Plan of the book

Chapter 2 starts by presenting the state of play and the agenda of the European Union, the most important player and centre of gravity in the region. The first part presents those policy areas that relate to irregular migration and asylum in Europe, and the strategies developed during the Tampere (1999–2004) and Hague (2005–10) Programmes: combating irregular migration and smuggling, migration management, border control, the maritime aspect of migration management, asylum and return. Reference is made to the question of burden-sharing among member states, its necessity and challenges. The agenda seems to have gradually shifted from unilateral control to more bilateral and regional cooperation and mainstreaming of migration in development and the Union's relations with third countries. Transit migration is not spelled out as a policy point to be addressed, yet the policies mentioned above affect its presence and evolution. It is argued that the lack of an established admissions policy in Europe remains a major shortcoming in the effort to prevent irregular and transit migration.

The second part of this chapter concentrates particularly on the external dimension of the EU migration and asylum policy in relation to the two neighbouring regions in question, North Africa and the former Soviet republics. This section examines the way in which migration management is incorporated in the Union's external relations with its neighbours, the partnerships developed and the work conducted in the area of capacity building. In addition, the section presents the current trend of mainstreaming migration policy with the Union's foreign and development policy with third countries, the so-called 'global approach to migration'. Reference is made to most recent EU policy proposals to combine admissions for third-country nationals with a broader migration-development package. In relation to asylum, the concepts of extra-territorial processing and regional protection programmes are closely related to transit migration. I also examine the concept of 'externalization', which has proven very popular in academic and migration debates, even though often overstated or misleading.

Staying on the inside of European borders, Chapter 3 focuses on the case of transit migration in Greece. The country displays a paradox of being both a preferred destination for some and a transit step for other migrants, particularly refugees. Transit migration is created and sustained by weak migration policies, a continuous state reluctance and neglect, an unpromising asylum system, a repeated regularization pattern and a vast informal economy that presents work opportunities. Many refugees do not apply for asylum in Greece at all, hoping to obtain asylum elsewhere, a phenomenon that is a direct consequence of the shortcomings of the Dublin regulation. The country seems preoccupied with combating irregular migration at the borders; what happens after arrival with those living and working illegally is a non-issue. While generally negative, the locals display at the same time solidarity to transit refugees, mostly related to historical factors. This solidarity ideology coupled with the state's complete neglect provides a 'support structure' for the survival and mobilization of refugees in transit. Going back a few years to the mid-1990s when the first groups of asylum seekers from the Middle East arrived in Greece, one cannot help but notice that the policy of neglect has developed into a pattern – reception, deportation, or more commonly, neglect and invisible dispersal of the transit migrants and refugees in the country. The example of Greece is not unique. It is certain that many of these observations also apply to other Southern European member states sharing similar migration characteristics.

Chapter 4 shifts the focus from the state to the migrants and describes how the situation is experienced from their perspective. I start by examining the journey from the Middle East through Turkey to Greece. The most common points of entry are by land, through the Greek–Turkish border, or by sea, with boats crossing from the Turkish coast to the Aegean islands. Using smugglers is very common and organized by small-scale, informal groups. Some migrants try to cross the border or the sea on their own, usually at great risk. Living conditions in the reception camps are very difficult, yet many end up staying for some time. Contrary to dominant impressions, few migrants have specific plans before leaving their homeland. Instead, it is while in transit that plans take shape. Living in transit is a condition of vulnerability and great anxiety, a state of being neither here nor there. Migrants and refugees live 'invisible' lives, work in the informal economy and save money for the future. Refugees are the most vulnerable groups among them, as access to asylum is hard and protection easily compromised. The situation described here is not unique, but typical of transit migrants and also holds for the other regions presented in this book.

In Chapter 5 I turn to another typical area of transit migration, the Maghreb. I examine the reasons that make North Africa a transit, and increasingly a destination space. Despite local specificities, certain characteristics are shared by all countries in the region, such as the increased participation of locals in the irregular and transit flows to Europe, substantial difficulties, lack of state capacities, reluctance to develop a policy framework and ostensible lack of interest in refugee protection. The EU factor is instrumental in the countries' policy responses. Despite the media hype about irregular migrants crossing from North Africa,

I argue that Europe is not the only region affected by transit migration; it is also North Africa itself. After all, those that stay behind are as many as those that cross the sea. The fact that refugees are also among those gathered in North Africa makes it imperative to provide asylum possibilities in the region. A chapter on North Africa would not be complete without special reference to Morocco. I analyse the condition of transit migration and asylum in Morocco, the 'support structures' that have developed and allow for migrant mobilization, and the way in which migration is instrumentalized in EU–Morocco relations. The 'externalization' discourse is particularly strong in relation to North Africa, employed commonly as a polemic against all sorts of interventions for capacity building, including those in support of refugees.

Moving from the southern to the eastern borders, Chapter 6 examines how the same condition has been experienced in Eastern Europe and the former Soviet republics in recent years. Contrary to the previous examples, transit migration in this part of the world is not only attributed to its vicinity to Europe. Instead, studies from the mid-1990s show that there was a long transit tradition with people moving between the former Soviet Republics, working and staying temporarily in various places, often closely related to studies or trade. To some extent, this continues to be the case today. Yet, the recent changes in the political landscape (collapse of communist regimes and the Soviet Union, accession of Central and Eastern European countries to the EU) have drastically modified that situation. Much of this previous mobility has become irregular as a result of new borders and new restrictions. Transit migration is prevalent in countries that provide work opportunities in the informal economy, such as Russia or Ukraine. Migrants and refugees in transit are no less vulnerable here than in other regions. What is more, irregular migration often overlaps with trafficking in this part of the world. As in North Africa, transit migrations also attract many locals who join in the same routes with the Asians going to Europe. National policies and institutions are also weak here, yet there seems to be a growing political interest and effort to build capacities and establish procedures for migration and asylum. Finally, the influence of the EU in this part of the world should be recognized as equally important, although it seems to have attracted less controversy in public discourse than in North Africa.

The last chapter brings together once again the main points in the analysis of transit migration and the examples presented in the book. I discuss the main characteristics of transit migration, its relation to irregular and regular migration and asylum, and its consequences for states and people. Transit migration is a phase that bears significant consequences for the countries – transit and destination – and the migrants themselves. Transit countries outside Europe face internal and external pressures to both combat irregular migration, and manage the migrant population resident in the country. Transit migration also has political ramifications in their relations with the European Union. Member states of the EU periphery, like Greece presented in this book, face the double challenge of being both host countries and at the same time Europe's gatekeeper, without, however, receiving the expected level of solidarity and support in order to fulfil this task. In addition, transit countries, both inside and outside of EU borders, are particularly reluctant to engage in asylum. Transit migration also has implications for 'traditional' destination countries in Europe in the long run. Many decisive steps in the process of migration to Western Europe are played out long before migrants reach these territories. Finally, the most significant aspect of transit migration is perhaps the impact that this condition has on the migrants and refugees themselves: the vulnerability, invisibility and social exclusion, the risks to human life, and ambiguity of protection often make this condition a risk to human security. Most of the time, migrants and refugees in transit survive through informal means, strategies and contacts. The time spent in transit is frequently time being wasted with the rebuilding of the migrant's life put on hold.

2
Migration in Europe

2.1   European migration and asylum policy

Almost all European countries are destination countries today. Immigration to Europe is growing in scope and complexity, and has a significant impact across different policy sectors. Irregular migration in particular is a major challenge, posing a number of security issues for states, and more importantly, for the migrants themselves. While it is hard to say with certainty how many migrants reside and work illegally in Europe today, the Council of Europe estimates that there are over 5.5 million irregular migrants living in the European Union (CoE, 2007). It is worth noting that those who enter illegally are few compared to those many more that arrive through regular channels, with a valid visa, and then overstay.

Moreover, in 2006 Europe was also host to 1,733,000 refugees and 199,000 new asylum seekers. Violence in Iraq has led thousands of people to seek asylum in the West, which in 2007 reached unprecedented numbers. It is estimated that in 2007 around 60,000 people have been fleeing the country each month. The most popular destinations are Sweden and Greece, followed by France, Britain and Canada. Neighbouring Syria was hosting 1.5 million displaced Iraqis at the end of September 2007 (UNHCR, 2007a).

This chapter will examine the policy framework for migration and asylum in Europe as developed up to the time of writing at the end of September 2007. The aim of this chapter is to provide the overall policy framework within which transit migration can be analysed and understood in the following chapters. While no EU policy consciously targets transit migration, all the policies that will be developed in this chapter have a direct and very real impact on the phenomenon.

Following an overview of policy developments during the Tampere (1999–2004) and Hague (2005–10) programmes, I will examine in particular policies that relate most closely to transit migration in peripheral member states and neighbouring countries, such as labour migration and admissions policy , the policies against irregular migration, the development of a common asylum policy, the concept and mechanisms of burden sharing, and the external dimension of migration and asylum policy in relation to transit and origin countries. The common thread that runs through all these policies in relation to transit migration is the lack of coherence that is reflected in weak harmonization and strong divergence between member states' national policies and practices. This divergence inevitably makes some countries more attractive destinations for migrants and refugees than others. On the other hand, however, open internal borders make movement between member states – regular or irregular – much easier. As a result, migrants and refugees tend to stay in transit and move between member states in search of the best opportunities for settlement and protection.

Furthermore, the lack of coherence is also reflected in a strong emphasis on control, but a weak interest in admissions and recruitment to meet the continent's labour market needs. Member states have been, on the one hand, particularly keen to strengthen border controls and collaborate with origin and transit countries in order to keep irregular migrants out. Yet on the other hand, they have not been as forthcoming in developing a common approach to a labour admissions policy. At the same time, the number of persons that hope to migrate to Europe in search of economic or political stability and protection continues unabated. As a result, an increasing number of migrants end up staying in transit in the neighbouring regions, waiting for the possibility to enter Europe illegally. It is only recently that the idea of a comprehensive approach has taken a step forward, with the hope of bridging such gaps and developing a more coherent policy both internally and externally.

Migration entered the harmonization agenda in the mid 1990s through the Amsterdam Treaty but it wasn't until the Tampere European Council that the aims and objectives were set for a common policy. Tampere set the following visionary objectives: a comprehensive approach to migration management, a fair treatment for third-country nationals, promotion of integration policies, partnerships with countries of origin including policies of co-development, and a common policy for asylum.

In the five years that spanned the Tampere programme, the European Union may not have reached these objectives, but it took a number of decisive steps and set certain EU-wide laws that laid the foundation for a common policy to be developed in the future. It also contributed towards developing an understanding of the need to build joint actions in the years to come. The debate on labour migration was initiated in 2001 by a Communication on a community immigration policy, and a consequent one on the conditions of entry and residence of third-country nationals for employment in Europe. Both documents set rather ambitious goals at the time, but were not followed up by any concrete actions during the Tampere Programme. Instead, the first steps were taken in relation to the migrant population already resident in Europe, and agreed on a Directive on the status of third-country nationals who are long-term residents and a Directive on the right to family reunion. The external dimension of EU migration policy picked up only during the last years of the Tampere Programme. The 2003 Thessaloniki Summit advanced the Union's work in the area of prevention and control of irregular migration. Following Thessaloniki, a Communication was published on the links between legal and illegal migration, namely the ways in which legal migration channels can reduce irregular migration pressures and be part of cooperation agreements with the countries of origin.[1] The Communication makes reference to quotas and the use of bilateral agreements between the EU and third countries.

The Hague programme presented in 2004 pushed the agenda further in a number of areas, most notably in the external dimension, the relation between migration and development, and integration. Its primal aim has been to provide a direction and framework for action in migration and asylum after enlargement, gradually moving towards harmonization. In addition, Hague placed emphasis on the guarantee of fundamental rights and access to justice, the fight against organized crime and terrorist threats. Hague includes a number of important steps towards building a common asylum policy and unified status in the Union.

Realizing its importance for the overall management of migration and the sustainability of European markets, Hague took up the issue of labour migration and ways to establish legal migration channels to Europe. A Green Paper on economic migration was presented in 2004, followed by a Policy Plan on Legal Migration (December 2005).[2] This Plan, a blueprint for policy steps in the coming years, amongst other things brings temporary migration schemes back to the table, and suggests 'multi-entry' visas for migrants staying temporarily who will return to their homeland and then re-migrate. Nevertheless, the key issue of admissions has proven too difficult to be agreed on by member states and one where they are most keen on maintaining their national approach. For this reason, the Commission proposes that states preserve the right to determine the number of migrants that can enter their country. It remains to be seen whether, and in what form, a migrant admissions policy will eventually be agreed in the Union. At the same time, certain aspects of admission advance faster, namely a framework safeguarding the rights of migrant workers and the admission of highly qualified migrants, set on the agenda for 2007–8. A framework for the admission for seasonal employment, remunerated trainees and intra-corporate transferees is also expected to be presented in 2008 (Frattini, 2007).

It is not certain to what extent the results expected by 2010 will actually be reached. Some argue that the Hague programme is too ambitious to be implemented by 2010, as member states are most likely to insist on their national agendas (van Selm, 2005a). It seems likely that a truly common policy will see the light in the course of a third programme after 2010. Many of the member states' policies do seem to go in a similar direction of increasing emphasis on control and restrictive migration and asylum policy. Nonetheless, as long as immigration policies differ within the Union certain countries are bound to receive more migrants and refugees than others. In addition, as long as there is no established Europe-wide admissions policy, EU border countries and neighbours will continue receiving the lion's share of irregular and transit migration. In contrast, the establishment of a structured framework for admissions and recruitment would provide migrants with a more specific destination and reduce the time that is now spent in transit.

Irregular migration and border control

While legal migration is difficult to agree on, the need to combat irregular migration seems to attract much broader enthusiasm. Irregular migration remains a major facet of transit migration. Any policy development that impacts irregular migration will also impact the transit dimension. During the Tampere programme, the focus was on how to prevent the illegal flows and stays in the member states rather than on how to tackle the causes and provide alternatives to illegal migration. A 'Proposal for a comprehensive plan to combat illegal immigration and trafficking' published in 2002 was the first truly comprehensive set of policy recommendations.[3] The proposal touched upon all areas related to irregular migration and sets the basis for the Commission's approach in the years to come; from uniform visa policy to joint control of external borders, from cooperation with third countries to re-admission agreements, from penalties for smugglers and traffickers to sanctions against illegal employment, everything was in there to serve as a blueprint. This proposal also foresaw a scoreboard and annual monitoring and evaluation mechanism. Nevertheless, not much action was taken in this area and member states continued with their national strategies in the following years.

The framework for combating smuggling and illegal entry in the Union was set through a Directive defining the facilitation of unauthorized entry, transit and residence and a Framework Decision on the penal framework to prevent these activities in November 2002.[4] Member states are asked to introduce sanctions that are effective, proportionate and dissuasive. The decision makes explicit reference to safeguarding access to protection for refugees and asylum seekers in accordance with international law.

With regards to border control, the Tampere programme focused on strengthening surveillance and control of external borders. As a result, migrants en route to the EU find it increasingly difficult to cross its borders, and stay for longer periods of time in transit outside the Union's borders. Tampere foresaw the setting up of an executive agency for the management of external borders, the EU border management agency (FRONTEX) which was created in 2005, during the Hague programme. The Hague programme gave new impetus to these efforts by allocating resources to improve burden sharing, such as ARGO funding for sharing control operations of external borders and a Community Fund for the Management of External Borders that is soon to be set up. The aim is to have mechanisms and instruments in place for joint actions and the use of technology in border control. In addition, the Commission has also proposed the creation of Rapid Border Intervention Teams (RABITs) composed of national border guards that will be available to assist member states facing situations of particular pressure, especially in cases of mass arrivals of irregular migrants. In addition to the support provided to member states, numerous joint operations involving EU and North African countries were conducted in 2006–7, such as the 'Hera II' in the Canary Islands and the Moroccan and Mauritanian coast, 'Nautilus', 'Poseidon' and 'Agios' in the Mediterranean, and the ARGO-funded 'Gate to Africa' operation. Most operations covered both maritime control and search and rescue purposes.

They are based on a pool of joint resources by member states and run in cooperation with the authorities of the neighbouring countries in North and West Africa. FRONTEX has also been involved in preparing risk analyses and feasibility studies, such as the MEDSEA, a study for the establishment of national coordination centres for control in the Mediterranean member states and third countries, or the BORTEC, a feasibility study for the establishment of a surveillance system covering the Mediterranean.

The creation of FRONTEX and the development of mechanisms for operational support and joint actions in the management of the Union's external borders have been seen by some as the consolidation of the European Union's security approach to migration. Europe is seen as a fortress that is now building an 'army' to keep the migrants out. Rather than questioning the need and purpose of a border management agency and strategy, the question should be to examine whether this has been happening in place of, or at the expense of, labour migration and asylum policy in Europe. In other words, border management could effectively work in tandem with a policy that welcomes labour migrants and refugees. In addition, and as the UNHCR '10-Point Plan of Action' suggested, there are ways to integrate refugee protection into migration and border control policies.[5] Regrettably, member states have not been as keen to advance their commitment in migration and asylum as they have been in the area of border control.

In parallel, the Hague programme has complemented the Union's approach to migration management through a more comprehensive understanding of the phenomenon encompassing push and pull factors and development. In particular, two Communications published in 2006 provide an overall description of the EC approach to irregular migration and ways to address it: the EU Communication on Illegal migration (July 2006), and the Communication 'The global approach to migration one year on: towards a comprehensive European migration policy' (November 2006).[6]

The July Communication proposes to increase exchange of information between member states on regularization programmes and combat employment of illegally residing third-country nationals. Building on a number of past Communications, this document brings a number of interesting additional features; most notably it is governed by a set of fundamental principles designed to guide EU actions, such as solidarity between member states, respect for fundamental rights, respect for the right to asylum, partnership with third countries, and setting clear rules for legal migration channels. The Communication also puts forward the need to cut down on illegal hiring and minimize abuse in the labour market.

The November Communication is a follow up to the concept of a 'global approach to migration' introduced in 2005, described in detail in the next section. The Communication focuses particularly on Africa – reflecting the most recent growing flows of irregular migration across the Mediterranean and the broader EU–Africa debate on migration that has been developing in the last couple of years. The Communication proposes to counter the problem by creating jobs in Africa and giving employment possibilities for African skilled persons to work in Europe. The two documents are characterized by greater sensitivity to the risks that migrants face when trying to reach Europe.

Another important strand in the Hague programme is the mainstreaming of migration into the Union's foreign and development relations with third countries. The topic strikes at the heart of the transit migration *problematique* and will be discussed in further detail in the next section.

Illegal hiring and informal labour practices are a major factor that attracts and sustains irregular and transit migration. It took a number of years to shift the policy focus from the prevention of illegal entries at the borders to illegal labour practices inside the host countries. After the July 2006 Communication, a proposal for a Directive on harmonized sanctions against employers who hire irregular migrants was adopted in May 2007.[7] The proposed directive aims to reduce the pull factor of illegal hiring and enhance law enforcement in this area. While a necessary policy measure, the proposed directive seems to take a narrow approach to the issue, focusing almost exclusively on the employers and on how to reduce illegal hiring, without paying any particular attention to the vulnerability and exploitation of migrants (Carrera and Guild, 2007).

Finally, the Hague programme places new emphasis on return. The debate on return was initiated in 2002 through the Green Paper on return that aimed to set common definitions and standards on return, expulsion, detention and removal. A Proposal for a directive was presented in September 2005.[8] Generally speaking, return of illegally residing migrants is an essential law enforcement and management component for the function and credibility of migration policy. It also helps gain legitimacy for admissions. Similarly, voluntary return of asylum seekers is one of the three preferred and durable refugee solutions. A return policy is essential in order to safeguard the value of refugee protection, combat asylum abuse and restore the credibility of the asylum system for governments and the public. The essential condition remains that return is voluntary, feasible and sustainable. The proposal gives priority to voluntary return 'to all extents possible', while forced return of asylum seekers may be necessary 'as a last resort'. On the other hand, the proposal seems to be more preoccupied with enforcing the return of third-country nationals who are illegally resident than supporting voluntary return. A Return Fund is also planned to be established soon. The European Parliament and the European Economic and Social Committee (EESC) have criticized the Union's eagerness to implement a European return and exclusion policy at a time when common migration legislation and legal migration channels are still under formation; in the EESC words 'it is like putting the cart before the horse' (EESC, 2002).

Migrants and refugees at sea

Numerous tragic events in the Mediterranean during the past few years have attracted public attention to the maritime aspect of migration management. The number of persons attempting to cross the Mediterranean to Italy, Greece, Malta and Spain or the Atlantic to the Canaries has increased, and the flow continues. Even though the majority of migrants found in the sea are usually rescued or intercepted and brought to shore, a smaller number of them perish. In fact, seen in perspective, the number of irregular migrants arriving by sea is only a small proportion of the total of migrants arriving illegally in Europe. While it is not known how many persons successfully manage to cross, it is estimated that 7270 have died in the sea since 1988 and another 3642 are still missing.[9] The maritime aspect of irregular migration is closely related to transit migration. It is one of the aspects in the course of movement that render migrants most vulnerable. Successful management and coordinated efforts between destination and transit countries could reduce the risks posed to human lives, safety and protection.

Interception and rescue operations are usually based on national migration and maritime policies which still differ between member states. There are also a number of international maritime conventions that set the overall standards and principles governing search and rescue operations.[10] These set the rules for the responsibilities of shipmasters to render assistance for rescue and disembarkation, and the corresponding responsibilities of the states, as well as the need to safeguard the principle of non-refoulement for persons in need of protection. The conventions foresee assistance to all persons found in distress at sea, 'regardless of the nationality or status' (SAR Convention,

Chapter 2.1.10). The search and rescue regime is at the intersection between international maritime law and international refugee law, bringing together different policy and legal areas: the right to life, as enshrined in international human rights; the right to seek asylum; the law of the sea defining areas of responsibility and competences in national and international waters; border control and the fight against illegal immigration, as developed through national policies and EU common actions; and the fight against smuggling and the Palermo Protocols.

An important obstacle is the fact that states do not always agree to disembarkation. The Guidelines on the Treatment of Persons Rescued at Sea (2004) suggest that the government responsible for the Search and Rescue (SAR) region in which survivors were recovered is responsible for providing a 'place of safety'. Yet, while responsibility is clear in the case of people intercepted or rescued in territorial waters, there seems to be confusion, and often disagreement, between states as to responsibility outside the territorial waters of the state intercepting or rescuing the boat. Disagreements have often led to migrants being stranded at sea for hours or days, as for example the case of migrants clinging for three days onto a tuna net in the Mediterranean as a result of a disagreement between Libya and Malta in June 2007. Countries tend to avoid disembarkation fearing that this might create a precedent and increase the number of arrivals in the future.

In addition, not all countries have ratified the amendments to the SAR Convention, adopted in 2006, which are the ones that essentially aim to relieve shipmasters of the responsibility to care for the survivors. Malta, for example, has not ratified the amendments to SAR. Its main concern is that ratifying will mean a substantial increase in the intake of boats for Malta, as it would become obliged to allow boats from further afield to disembark.[11] Taking into account the fact that Libya's SAR region still remains undefined, it is no surprise that Malta is not keen on the SAR Convention amendments.

A key issue is ensuring access to refugee protection for persons in need. According to the Guidelines on the Treatment of Persons Rescued at Sea (2004) disembarkation of asylum seekers and refugees in territories where their lives and freedom would be threatened should be avoided (Paragraph 6.17). Obviously, this would include the countries of origin or those from which the individuals have fled.

While no European policy framework is yet developed in the area of interception and rescue for migrants at sea, the interest seems to be growing. The Commission recently published a study on the international law instruments in relation to illegal migration by sea.[12] It suggested the drafting and agreement on EU guidelines that will complement UN rules on maritime law for the European member states in particular, and the adoption of common rules that will clarify which country is responsible for saving illegal migrants at sea. Maritime rescue operations need to be governed by a burden-sharing mentality; search and rescue operations need to be facilitated through coordination, joint bilateral and regional efforts, and pooling of resources to help save migrants at sea.

Public perceptions commonly see a causal relation between control and surveillance operations – national, and particularly joint EU operations – and rescue of migrants in distress at sea. In fact, though they may relate closely, they are rather different. FRONTEX for example, which provides support for control and surveillance measures undertaken by member states, is sometimes criticized for not providing rescue to migrants at sea. Yet, FRONTEX is not a European Coastal Patrol and has no such mandate. On the other hand, considering that the number of accidents and deaths at sea in the last years coincides with an intensification of maritime patrols, it is questioned whether increased surveillance and interception also increase deaths. For example, during the 1990s when sea patrols between Albania and Apulia increased, the number of accidents and casualties also increased, as migrants were trying to escape apprehension (European Parliament, 2006a). While this does not lead to any state responsibility, it does trigger the state's positive obligation to take preventive measures to safeguard human lives.

A common asylum policy

EU asylum policy is one of the areas having the most direct relation and impact on transit migration. The current asylum policy framework is one of the reasons why refugees remain in transit in peripheral member states and neighbouring countries; it is also one of the main factors affecting the length of transit stay, the course of movement between countries and the gradual settlement in a country.

In the process of EU harmonization of migration and asylum policy, the objective to establish a Common Asylum System was already set at Tampere, but it remains to be completed in the years to come. Tampere's main contribution to asylum policy was that it produced the first set of legally binding EU-level agreements: the Reception Conditions Directive, the Asylum Procedures Directive, the Qualification Directive and the Dublin Regulation.[13]

The Reception Conditions Directive sets minimum standards for the reception of asylum seekers across Europe, making specific reference to housing, education and health. The Qualification Directive sets the criteria that apply for a person to qualify either for refugee or subsidiary protection status and the rights attached to each status; it also sets a harmonized regime for subsidiary protection in the EU for those persons who fall outside the scope of the Geneva Convention, but who still need international protection, such as victims of generalized violence (non-state actors) or civil war. The Procedures Directive ensures that all refugee status determination procedures at the first instance are subject to the same minimum standards in all member states. These three directives set a series of standards which, if implemented using the same denominator, could in theory prevent 'asylum shopping' within the Union and safeguard the rights of refugees and asylum seekers.

Nevertheless, national asylum systems continue to display great divergence in Europe. Member states have transposed the directives, often taking the minimum standards as a benchmark, and even so national practices are frequently below standards. In July 2007 the Commission issued a reasoned opinion on the non-transposition of the qualifications directive; seven member states had not transposed it, while three others had incorporated it only partially.[14]

Material reception conditions vary greatly from one country to another and access to the labour market for asylum seekers is not uniform. Integration programmes for refugees, including language courses, social welfare, vocational training and recognition of their qualifications, are also diverse, with some member states lagging substantially behind. These differences are some of the main factors leading to transit migration in the European Union: as we shall see in the example of Greece, asylum seekers are discouraged from staying in Greece because reception conditions are particularly bad. As a result, they prefer to remain undocumented. At the same time, access to employment gives them the possibility to sustain a livelihood while in transit. In addition, further differences between member states also account for the reasons that push refugees to move and stay in transit. These are differences in the criteria applied for someone to qualify for refugee or subsidiary forms of protection, differences in the rights granted to refugees and asylum seekers, and the national procedures for refugee status determination.

The Reception Conditions and Qualification Directive are to be evaluated and reviewed by 2010. The Long-Term Residents Directive for labour migrants is being amended to include refugees in its scope. A Green Paper on the future Common European Asylum System (CEAS) was published in June 2007, to be followed by a Policy Plan on Asylum policy.[15] The main objective of CEAS would be to achieve a common asylum procedure and a uniform status valid throughout the Union. The Green Paper asks for higher common standards of protection, a fairer system and greater solidarity between member states.

A Common European Asylum System would involve a lot more than a revision of what is currently available in terms of legal framework and administrative cooperation. The actual model of such a system is still under discussion at the time of writing, and it will be up to the member states to decide whether this should take the form of a centralized EU structure for decision making and reception, or the strengthening of the existing Community institutions to monitor implementation at national level. A uniform status would mean uniform eligibility criteria for the granting of refugee status, harmonization of rights and benefits available to refugees and a harmonized status for persons in need of complementary forms of protection or the like. It would also need a community mechanism for the mutual recognition of national asylum decisions and the possibility to transfer protection responsibilities from one member state to the other. Practical cooperation between administrations would need to be substantially intensified in order to achieve convergence between national systems. Plans are on the table to set up a European Asylum Support Office, linked to the Commission, as a central unit to assist all forms of cooperation, provide training and support in areas of particular pressure, and monitor reception conditions in member states. A common asylum policy would contribute greatly to reducing the need for transit migration within the EU. Asylum seekers would no longer have to remain in transit after they cross the Union's borders, while hoping to reach a different EU destination where they might increase their chances of receiving protection. The particularly vulnerable position of asylum seekers and refugees makes it all the more important to remove the insecurity inherent in transit migration.

Sharing the burden

Burden-sharing is one of the policy areas that could address and prevent transit migration more efficiently, both between member states and between the Union and third countries. Noll's (2000) scholarly approach to burden-sharing in the European Union sees three forms: sharing the policies (harmonization and uniform refugee status and subsidiary protection), sharing the resources and costs, and sharing the number of beneficiaries. While a common asylum policy is still in the making, member states have already been sharing some costs through the European Refugee Fund (ERF) that finances refugee reception and integration projects at local and national level. The first round of programmes was completed in 2000–4, while a second round is now running for 2005–10. The example of Greece presented in Chapter 3 shows that the current system for the allocation of funds often fails to reflect the needs' real dimensions. The Finnish Presidency in 2006 proposed establishing a mechanism in order also to finance the processing of asylum applications in member states through EU funding.[16]

Sharing the refugees is more complicated. 'Physical' distribution has been applied in the case of temporary protection of Kosovars under the UNHCR Humanitarian Evacuation Programme (van Selm, 2000). It was first proposed by the German Presidency in 1994 in the context of mass displacement from the Balkans.[17] The German proposal suggested compulsory redistribution of refugees on the basis of the countries' population, size of territory and GDP. It was opposed, however, by countries that in the past received few refugees, and by others who claimed that a compulsory distribution was potentially violating the refugees' human rights and consent (Thielemann, 2003). The current revision of the Long-Term Residents Directive to include refugees is also expected to alleviate the burden on certain member states by allowing those persons, under certain conditions, to move to another member state.

Scholars have also proposed the possibility of 'soft' resettlement as an alternative that is non-binding for member states and depends on 'double voluntarism' – the condition that both the recipient country and the refugee agree before resettlement takes place (Boswell, 2003). Such a mechanism is already included in the Directive on temporary protection. In general, resettlement would be an important solidarity mechanism, and is one of the three durable solutions for displaced persons (the other two being local integration and voluntary return). The possibility of an EU-wide resettlement scheme has been on the table since 2003. It is usually included in the debates in relation to Regional Protection Programmes (see below). A resettlement scheme should be complementary to and not alternative to processing of spontaneous applications in the Union (van Selm et al., 2003). Certain member states have been involved in resettlement before; the rest seem to lack the political will to engage.

In addition, the Green Paper on CEAS poses the question of whether it is appropriate and feasible to have joint processing of asylum applications in the Union, as a means of further harmonization. Advocates of the redistribution policy claim that this would be the most effective way of burden-sharing, as states will also equalize non-quantifiable costs. Nevertheless, it is not certain how far sharing the refugees is pragmatic and feasible, and it may also not be fair. Ideally, a common asylum policy offering uniform status and reception conditions would eventually provide the best guarantees. Operational support could be made available to member states through, for example, 'asylum expert teams' as suggested by the European Commission and the UNHCR, in order to address urgent needs at points of arrival.

A policy closely linked to the distribution of refugees – even though initially not designed as such – is the Dublin system. The Dublin system, introduced through the Dublin Convention in 1997 and revised through the Dublin Regulation (Dublin II) in 2003, sets the rules about the member state that should be responsible for handling an asylum application. Its stated aim is to prevent multiple asylum claims in member states and avoid refugees being stranded in the Union. According to the Regulation, the first member state entered by the asylum seeker (legally or illegally) is responsible for examining the asylum application according to its national law, and is also obliged to take back its applicants who are irregularly in another member state. A special clause called the 'Sangatte clause' (Gil-Bazo, 2006) relieves member states from their responsibility in case another member state proves to be responsible for their unlawful stay, provided the person stayed undetected for at least five months.

Nevertheless, the system has created excessive reception challenges on peripheral states that are the first points of arrival, leading to refugees in transit in the Union. It is estimated that 15 per cent of the 237,840 applications submitted in the EU in 2005 were subject to determination of responsibility under Dublin II (UNHCR, 2006), which shows that a proportion of asylum seekers entered Europe through one country, but then continued the journey and sought asylum in another or in both. This number does not, however, include the undetected, which would certainly make up for a much higher percentage in total. It is telling that in 2006 the Maltese Minister for the Interior asked for derogation from the regulation, feeling that it places an unequal burden on the small island of 400,000 inhabitants (European Parliament, 2006c). The Dublin system seems to ignore that member states are not only of different sizes but also different reception capacities, asylum policies and recognition rates. Essentially, the Dublin system has lead to the increase of irregular and transit migration, as persons in need of protection usually prefer to remain undocumented in Greece, Italy, Spain or Poland, in order to apply for asylum in another member state. In some cases, it may even have provided certain member states with an incentive not to develop adequate reception systems, in the hope that asylum seekers will therefore prefer to continue their journey further. More specific examples of these practices are detailed in the following chapters. In addition, member states frequently deny access to asylum to individuals transferred under the Dublin system, putting refugees at risk of forced return. It is worth noting that only 30 per cent of the identified and 'accepted' Dublin cases are consequently transferred from one member state to another (UNHCR, 2006). Nobody knows what happens with the rest. The asylum case is often interrupted after departure and is not reopened if the refugee is requested to return to the first member state; instead, a Dublin transfer is usually followed by detention and deportation.

The Dublin system has received substantial criticism from the practitioners' world. The European Council for Refugees and Exiles (ECRE) assesses the system as unfair, inefficient, resource-intensive and an obstacle to genuine burden-sharing between European states. What is more, the system denies refugees a fair hearing and puts them at risk, only adding further to their suffering (ECRE, 2007). ECRE proposed amending the system in such a way that responsibility for the asylum application would be with the member state where the asylum seeker either has family (and agrees to join), or has first lodged an application, providing that there are no risks of returning there (ECRE, 2006). On the contrary, the Commission in its evaluation of the Dublin system concluded that the objectives 'to establish a clear and workable mechanism for determining responsibility for asylum applications have, to a large extent, been achieved'.[18] The issue is now re-examined as part of the debate on a Common European Asylum System.

The first section has presented the main strands of policy developments in the area of migration and asylum policy in Europe since the Tampere Summit and up to the present that relate most closely to the phenomenon of transit migration. Looking ahead towards 2010, when the Hague programme is expected to reach its completion, the development of an admissions policy and the opening of legal migration channels for skilled and unskilled migrant workers will be a fundamental step forward in combating irregular migration and preventing abuse, exploitation and risk to human lives. The framework for the management of the Union's external borders is an important step that nevertheless needs to be enhanced with humanitarian and refugee protection components and become more comprehensive. The maritime aspect of migration control – search and rescue operations – needs to be further strengthened and included in the Union's overall approach to migration and asylum. The development of a common European asylum system, including a uniform protection status and comparable reception and protection standards across the Union, is perhaps among the most crucial points; such a system could prevent secondary movements of refugees who spend some time living in transit in one member state and then look for protection in another. A workable system of burden-sharing is urgently needed, in order to balance out the inequitable distribution and challenges posed on peripheral member states, and allow them to respond to refugee needs with ethical commitment rather than with resentment for the 'burden'.

An equally important aspect in the analysis of the phenomenon of transit migration is the external dimension of European migration and asylum policy, and the ways in which the Union works with origin and transit countries in this area, as described in the next section.

2.2   The external dimension of EU migration and asylum policy

The demand for immigration into the EU is much greater than the opportunities for legal entry that are on offer. In recent years, most EU member states have been reluctant to open many channels of legal entry. At the same, policies relating to the control of the EU's external borders are much more robust. This has led to a growing pool of asylum seekers and migrants who are trying (or trying again) to enter the EU. The external dimension of EU migration and asylum policy is the approach through which migration and asylum issues relate to the Union's broader political relations and cooperation with third countries that are origin and transit countries. It is also the policy framework within which transit migration in the Union's neighbouring regions can be understood.

The High Level Working Group on Migration and Asylum (HLWG), established by the Council in 1998, was the first policy step in this direction. The HLWG drew Action Plans aiming to address the root causes of migration from six countries/regions of origin: Morocco, Sri Lanka, Somalia, Afghanistan, Iraq and Albania/Kosovo. The Action Plans were adopted by the Council in 1999 and 2000. The HLWG also helped coordinate efforts between the Community, the UNHCR and member states to assist third countries in dealing with the refugees on their territory. Despite this rather pioneering start, the next years saw a gradual 'securitization' of the topic, particularly in the Seville Summit (2002) which shifted the emphasis on readmission agreements and advocated for 'negative conditionality' in the Union's relations with third countries. In the next years the concept of the 'external dimension' of migration policy evolved into something broader and beyond the readmission agreements, towards that of 'partnerships' with third countries. In 2005 the first external strategy of Justice, Freedom and Security was officially articulated.[19] Amongst other things it highlighted that 'the EU's attempts to create an area of freedom, security and justice can only be successful if they are underpinned by a partnership with third countries to strengthen the rule of law and promote human rights and the respect for international obligations.'

By 'partnerships', what is understood here is working together with source and transit countries in the short and medium term in order to manage migration. The fight against irregular migration – strengthening border controls, improving travel document security and fighting human smuggling and trafficking – is only one of the components in this partnership. A clause on readmission agreements is inevitably included in cooperation, and so will a future return policy. Enhancing protection and durable solutions for refugees in regions of origin and transit is another item on the agenda of partnerships that gradually gains more and more attention and funding.

Recently, the external dimension of migration and asylum policy is being reshaped by a gradual mainstreaming of migration in the Union's policy areas, instruments and administrations involved with third countries, and a closer association between migration and development. In addition, in the framework of its existing relations the EU advocates for countries to adopt and implement the relevant international standards and obligations relating to migrants and refugees. Partnership also means providing the means in order for third countries to be in a position and capacity to cooperate, through technical and financial assistance and capacity building.

An important point to clarify is the difference between the external dimension of migration policy on the one hand, and the 'externalization' of migration policy on the other. The externalization concept is commonly used in the academic and policy worlds, and usually attracts heated debates. Its supporters interpret the involvement of migration in external relations as a method employed by the EU to 'export' and shift its responsibilities outside its territory, rather than as an integral part of development cooperation. Geddes (2005), for example, speaks of the 'outsourcing' of EU migration and asylum policy to Morocco and Libya (see also Schuster, 2005a; Andrijasevic, 2006; Goldschmidt, 2006; and others). Nevertheless, 'externalization' arguments are in most cases based on a partial assessment or knowledge of the situation prevailing on the ground in third countries, and a simplified understanding of the types of cooperation actions developed between these countries and European or other international actors. It is commonly argued, for example, that the support provided by the EU and international organizations to third countries in order to develop their legislative framework and build a system for refugee protection is not capacity building to meet actual needs, but rather a way to 'burden' them with Europe's unwanted refugees. To a large extent this assessment stems from a general confusion about the aims and objectives of capacity building in transit countries, as well as negligence about the needs of refugees living in these countries and the states' obligations to deliver refugee protection. The 'externalization' theory tends to contribute to nurturing a hype and suspicions about a burden-shifting scenario, without, however, bringing any constructive conclusions about how partnerships should be built, what needs third countries might be facing, or how the funding available could be used to meet them.

The Union tends to develop regional approaches for cooperation in relation to established regional entities, even though the approach to each country is also tailor-made to its characteristics. The following sections examine how migration and asylum policy is integrated in the Union's relations with its immediate neighbours that are both origin and transit countries, and consequently with the rest of the developing world. It will provide the necessary background for the understanding of transit migration and policy developments in the South and East, developed in the relevant chapters.

Migration and European Neighbourhood Policy

Following European Commission President Prodi's declaration, and a series of preparatory discussions and documents, the European Neighbourhood Policy was eventually adopted in 2004. One of its main objectives was to bring cooperation with all of the EU's neighbours – East and South – under one unique policy framework and financial instrument to create a belt of prosperity, security and stability around Europe. The policy was given financial clout with the adoption of the

European Neighbourhood Policy Instrument (ENPI) that, as of 2007, replaces MEDA and the other previous financial instruments. For the implementation of the policy, Action Plans are negotiated with each individual country. This allows for countries that want to move faster towards a closer cooperation to do so. Compared to its other policies of international cooperation, the ENP foresees a much closer 'rapprochement' with the countries it covers, and allows for the use of cooperation instruments, such as twinning, originally reserved to enlargement countries.

Migration is currently seen as a key priority area in European Neighbourhood Policy. All national and regional strategy papers and Action Plans with partner countries include a JHA chapter on the following issues: asylum, migration, visa, readmission, border management, police and judicial cooperation, the fight against organized crime, human trafficking, drugs, financial and economic crime (in particular money laundering) and corruption. Up to 3 per cent of the ENPI budget is now earmarked for migration issues. To some extent, migration management with the neighbouring countries is gradually seen in the context of the 'Global Approach to Migration' that is currently being developed and fosters the mainstreaming of migration in external and development relations with third countries.

With regard to North Africa in particular, migration has already been included in the Barcelona process and the Association Agreements signed with each country for some time now, but it is only recently that it has started attracting such political attention. Today, and following flagship meetings such as the EU–Africa conference on migration in Rabat in July 2006, and the EU–Africa conference on migration and development in Tripoli in November 2006, migration management has become a key area in the partnerships. The emphasis is as much on the migration of Maghrebi nationals to Europe, as it is on migrants from other countries passing through this region on their way to Europe.

A large part of ENP funding is dedicated to programmes in North Africa, including migration programmes. Migration also features in MEDA bilateral and regional programmes, for example in the 'MEDA/JAI' Phase I regional programme that focused on migration, justice and police (2004–6) and included a 'MEDA/Migration' project on data collection and research. The 'MEDA/JAI' Phase II regional programme is announced to start in 2008. Other projects, particularly for capacity building and the fight against irregular migration, are also financed under instruments such as the B7-667 and the AENEAS.

Morocco, which has had an association agreement with the EU since 1996, is the leading beneficiary of community assistance in the Mediterranean. Various projects in the area of migration have taken place in the last few years, spanning technical and financial assistance for the management of border control, to programmes for Moroccans wishing to emigrate, and capacity building for the authorities in the area of migration and asylum. For example, a MEDA project has been promoting labour migration from Morocco to Europe and supporting the relevant agency in charge of recruitment, information on employment possibilities, training and return of migrants in the future. The amended Action Plan (2004) foresees amongst others the development of asylum legislation in accordance with international standards and the implementation of the relevant UN Refugee Convention and its Protocol. At the same time, the EU has also been negotiating a readmission agreement with Morocco for many years, but talks have been slow.

Cooperation with Tunisia and Algeria is similar, even though less extensive. The EU is negotiating a readmission agreement with Tunisia, and in 2006 it started discussions also with Algeria. Cooperation with Libya is on an ad hoc basis and does not follow the formal process of negotiation and partnership, as Libya is not part of the Barcelona process. Projects in the area of migration management are funded outside the budget dedicated for ENP, for example through the AENEAS programme. An Action Plan on illegal migration was proposed to Libya in 2006 following an emerging dialogue after the UK presidency in 2005, yet Libya did not agree to this type of collaboration.

Migration issues are also gaining momentum in the Union's relations with its eastern and south-eastern neighbours. In the Western Balkans migration is included in the Stabilization and Association Agreements negotiated and concluded with each of the countries individually. Aside from the return of the former Yugoslav Republics' own refugees, important items on the agenda are the fight against illegal migration and human trafficking, the strengthening of asylum legislation, implementation of the readmission agreements already signed with the EC, and implementation of Community visa facilitation agreements which have already started with some countries. Visa facilitation is a priority topic for the Western Balkans, as it also is for countries like Ukraine and Moldova. Cooperation on migration issues also takes place at various other regional initiatives in the Balkans, such as the South-East European Cooperation Process (SEECP) and the MARRI (Migration, Asylum and Refugees Regional Initiative).

With regard to the countries of Eastern Europe and the Southern Caucasus, migration and asylum issues are included in the Partnership and Cooperation Agreements and ENP Action Plans agreed with each of them. Some countries, like Ukraine, have a separate JHA national Action Plan as well. Dialogue and cooperation progress differs greatly from one country to another; Moldova and Ukraine seem particularly engaged in these issues. In contrast, relations with Belarus are not yet at the level of full-fledged partnership and cooperation on migration and border management is mostly concluded within the framework of regional programmes. While Action Plans are already signed with Armenia, Azerbaijan and Georgia, dialogue and cooperation on migration is still under formation. Readmission agreements are currently being negotiated. As far as Russia is concerned, a 'Road Map of the Common Space on Freedom, Security and Justice' was adopted in May 2005 in the context of the EU–Russia Partnership Cooperation Agreement (PCA). Finally, migration is also discussed with Kazakhstan, Uzbekistan and Kyrgyzstan in the framework of their PCA. No formal dialogue on migration exists yet with Turkmenistan and Tajikistan. The main assistance instrument is the TACIS, gradually also replaced by the ENPI, and the instrument for the non-ENPI countries, namely the Development Cooperation Instrument (DCI).

Migration and development

Mainstreaming migration in the Union's relations with third countries reflects a more comprehensive understanding of the relation between senders–receivers and migration push factors. This approach, which brings Justice, Freedom and Security closer together with the Union's Common Foreign and Security Policy, the European Security and Defence Policy, and the Union's policy in the area of development cooperation, was developed during 2005–6 and was particularly promoted by the UK Presidency of 2005. The external dimension strategy of JHA was also adopted during the same period.

The mainstreaming process has been articulated through the concept of 'Global Approach to Migration'. The 'Global Approach' includes all aspects of migration, from regular and irregular migration, smuggling and trafficking, to refugee protection, migrant rights, diasporas and remittances. This was first presented in a 2005 Communication on the challenges of migration.[20] A year later, a follow-up Communication was published in relation to Africa and the Mediterranean and further to that, a communication exploring ways to apply the Global Approach to the eastern and south-eastern third countries. The main objectives of the Global Approach are to address various migration issues through a coherent approach that brings together development, employment, migration management and external relations. The Global Approach is underscored by certain fundamental principles, namely partnership, solidarity and shared responsibility, and uses the concept of 'migratory routes' to develop and implement policy.

The link between migration and development in particular aims to address the structural factors that lead people to emigrate in the first place. Building strong governments and institutions in developing countries is fundamental to peace and stability and fighting poverty. Economic development and job creation is another key step in this direction. Relating migration to development is not only about less migration to Europe; it is also about more development in the countries of origin, through better migration management. The EU has been keen to highlight the role of remittances and diasporas in the development of home countries. Recently, attention has also been drawn to the possibility of temporary and circular migration schemes as a way to balance between migration and brain drain. This could take the form of short-stay visas or multi-entry visas giving migrants who return home the right to come back to Europe at a later stage. This proposal creates a bridge between development and admissions. Obviously, for this to happen, there should also be incentives and support for a meaningful and sustainable return. More importantly, there should also be the will from the receiving countries' side to give up on some of the benefits they have by recruiting (undocumented) labour from third countries. Castles (2006) argues that even in the form of voluntary circular migration, temporary migration programmes may be hard to materialize, since past experience shows that temporary migration most often becomes permanent, and also that labour market projections in Europe will require and sustain the presence of this migrant labour force in the future.

In relation to Africa in particular, new impetus in political dialogue and cooperation has been observed since 2005, as part of the broader debate on Africa and the EU Strategy for Africa. The EU Strategy for Africa, adopted by the European Council in December 2005, aims to meet the Millennium Development Goals and promote sustainable development, security and good governance in Africa. Cooperation on migration and development aims to create jobs in African countries, particularly in sectors with high outward migration, minimize irregular migration, maximize the benefits of diasporas and remittances, and reduce brain drain. At the same time, there is also increasing awareness among African states themselves of the importance of migration for the whole continent. This was also reflected in the African Union Common Position on Migration and Development endorsed in Banjul in July 2006, the EU–Africa Ministerial Conference on Migration and Development in Tripoli of November 2006, and the EU–Africa Ouagadougou Action Plan to combat human trafficking in 2006.

The ministerial Conference on migration and development in Rabat in July 2006 was a flagship meeting that created a new dynamic in this area. The Rabat Declaration and Action Plan by West, Central and North African and EU member states aimed to address the migratory route through West Africa. Substantial emphasis was placed on development, while issues such as human rights and refugee protection only featured as minor. A few months later, a second EU–Africa ministerial conference took place on Migration and Development in Tripoli, Libya. This conference gave substance to ideas of bridging migration partnerships and admissions and giving a more concrete and tangible form to cooperation for migration and development between North and South.

Moving from conceptual debates to practice, various proposals have been put forward for mechanisms that could support this approach. Gathering background information is the first step. A proposed measure is to create 'Migration Profiles' for each developing country, annexed to the Country Strategy Papers that will be collecting information and analysis to be used in the medium term in order to develop concrete measures for technical and financial assistance. Immigration Liaison Officers already posted in third countries could help with information and recommendations. The concept of 'migratory routes' was coined in 2006 as a way to make interventions comprehensive, by drafting Action Plans that bring together source and transit countries. For example, the Southern Migratory Route would include Northern and Sub-Saharan Africa, while the Eastern Migratory Route would involve Eastern Europe, the Russian Federation and Central Asia.

Supporting the countries' capacities is another important step. The Communication on Migration and Development proposes to create 'Migration Support Teams' consisting of experts from EU member states to provide assistance to requesting third countries.[21] 'Cooperation Platforms' could bring together third countries, EU member states and international organizations in the area of migration and development to ensure effective migration management for a country or a region, and along certain migratory routes. Another plan adopted is to create a 25 million euro 'Migration Capacity Building Facility' for third countries in Africa, the Caribbean and Pacific (ACP) that will monitor and study migration flows and support capacity-building activities.

The 2007 Communication on circular migration also presents the idea of creating 'Mobility Packages' with certain countries that could entail various measures; for example, a collection of labour migration quotas offered by different member states, information on vacancies in member states, favourable treatment for admission of the countries' nationals, and technical assistance such as job-matching services and preparation for departure.[22] Migration web portals could back these packages. These measures would also need to be supported by information campaigns in countries of origin to alert people to the dangers of irregular migration and the possible legal migration channels to Europe. A pilot 'Migration Information and Management Centre' is planned to be set up in Mali both to inform Malians about job and training opportunities at home and abroad and legal channels for temporary migration, and to support the capacities of the Malian institutions.[23]

The proposals in relation to eastern and south-eastern countries are similar, as presented in the relevant 2007 Communication.[24] Applying the 'Global Approach' to the East proposes similar measures, such as 'migration profiles' and 'cooperation platforms' on migration and development. For example, a cooperation platform for the Black Sea region – an area particularly important in terms of transit migration and trafficking – could be set up. Circular migration and facilitation of mobility of persons through partnerships and visa facilitation schemes would also be explored.

Certainly, the expansion of the EU agenda in all these directions shows a more comprehensive understanding of the phenomenon of international migration beyond a purely border control mentality. In terms of the actual measures proposed, these can be feasible in the medium term. Whether they are sustainable in the long run is not certain and will also depend on local specificities. Mainstreaming migration in external relations, foreign policy and development is a wise step to take, as it makes interventions in the area of migration more contextualized and coordinated. Policy interventions will also make better sense this way, making clear the relation between poverty, governance, labour market and migration. Such a comprehensive approach also touches upon transit migration not only by reducing the push factors of emigration, but also by addressing migration pressures and challenges in the transit countries through capacity building. The main challenge however remains that of implementation, which also depends on continued commitment from the side of both the EU and the beneficiary country/partner. The topics are jointly agreed with the beneficiary country, and partnership documents are drafted together and co-owned. Commitment is often not as straightforward as it seems, considering that partner countries often lack the capacity or fail to back their agreements with political will and practical action to absorb the funds allocated. Technical and financial assistance on actions jointly agreed also comes with conditions and responsibilities on the side of the receivers.

Other types of commitments expected are cooperation in readmission agreements, active awareness raising to discourage illegal migration, commitment to promote employment and decent work at home, enhanced border control and travel document security, and combating smuggling and trafficking. A readmission obligation for ACP countries is also foreseen in Article 13 of the Cotonou Agreement.

Partner countries often ask for incentives in return, one of the most popular being visa facilitation. At the same time, the EU should also be clear about its commitment that these developments will not divert its intention to open up legal channels for migration of third-country nationals and ensure access and delivery of protection to those in need.

Capacity building in transit countries

As mentioned, most of the interventions in transit countries neighbouring Europe are financed by the relevant geographical financial instruments. At the same time, and in order to allow for greater flexibility additional budget lines have been created to support action in third countries of origin and transit in the area of migration management. The first programme, known under its budget line number 'B7-667', was created in 2001 to provide financial and technical assistance for capacity building in migration management and the fight against smuggling and trafficking, strengthen international protection and asylum procedures in the transit countries, and assist with voluntary return and reintegration. With 49 small-scale projects in 2001–3 (totalling 42.5 million euro) this programme gave visibility to the external dimension of JHA, both in Europe and in the third countries, and initiated partnerships with a number of international organizations and small and medium-sized NGOs.

Its successor, 'AENEAS', was established in 2004 for the period 2004–8 (consequently shortened to the three years 2004–7) with a budget of 250 million. Following the same approach, AENEAS supported small-scale projects or pilot efforts for migration management and asylum in the regions, complementary to the geographical financial instruments, opting for both governmental and non-governmental implementing partners as a way to speed up and facilitate processes. It also provided funding possibilities for actions in countries where Country Strategy Papers or Indicative Programmes are not present, as for instance with Libya. To give an example, IOM is funded to carry out a project of capacity building for the Libyan authorities on migration and refugee law, training of border guards, research and assistance to voluntary return. There are about 67 such AENEAS projects currently being implemented.

The successor of AENEAS, the 'Thematic Programme for Cooperation with third countries in the field of asylum and migration' has been announced for 2007–10 (380 million euros) and 2010–13 (175 million euros).[25] The Programme aims to integrate migration and asylum into cooperation and development policy, in line with the mainstreaming approach that is currently evolving. It will also promote legal economic migration to Europe and the protection of the rights of migrants in third countries. The programme also picks up on the question of regional protection programmes that will be developed later in this chapter. This programme finally gives substance to the idea of 'migratory routes' mentioned earlier, allocating funds to the Southern, Eastern and Middle Eastern migratory routes and South–South migrations in particular.[26]

Protecting refugees in the transit countries

Asylum has been a particularly controversial topic within the external dimension of EU migration policy. It forms part of a debate that has been growing following a couple of proposals put forward by member states suggesting the screening of asylum applications outside the Union's borders. The proposals triggered a strong reaction from academics, practitioners and civil society as well as most member states. Even though they have been rejected and no similar proposal has been seriously discussed in recent years, they still continue to dominate the debate.

These proposals suggested ways to process asylum applications outside Europe, in order to prevent asylum seekers from entering the continent, known as 'extraterritorial processing.' Inspired by Australia's Pacific solution of offshore processing, the United Kingdom in 2003 proposed the idea of 'transit processing centres' (TPC) outside Europe, but the proposal was rejected at the Thessaloniki Council. In 2004 a new proposal in the same direction was tabled by Germany and Italy, to establish TPC in North Africa, and was similarly rejected by most member states. Essentially, both proposals would make fears of 'externalization' a reality: if implemented, they could indeed have been a way of 'outsourcing' the Union's asylum obligations and burdening other countries. Aside from being unacceptable on ethical grounds, such measures would also be legally questioned (Kneebone, 2005) and in any case practically unfeasible. Although they never materialized, the ripples created by these proposals still make it almost impossible today to discuss refugee protection in transit countries without raising suspicions of 'externalization' attempts.

Rather than debating at length policies that could have been but are not, we should instead shift our focus to the policies that have actually been adopted and constitute the Union's strategy in this field. In particular, the EU has tried to promote the possibility for refugees to find protection wherever they are in the transit regions. This concept is also expressed in Regional Protection Programmes.[27] The overall idea is to enhance the capacity of areas close to regions of origin so that they are in a position to protect refugees in their territory and promote durable solutions for refugees already residing in these countries. The approach is central to the issue of mixed flows and the refugees who are stranded or stuck in transit countries, unable to go back and often unable to continue the journey any further and seek asylum in Europe.

The neighbouring transit countries that are signatories to the international instruments for refugee protection have an international obligation to provide asylum to persons in need equal with that of European countries. This alone should suffice as a reason for the need to support the neighbouring transit countries in their efforts and obligation to offer asylum. In addition, the possibility of asylum in the transit countries would mean less people risking their lives every year trying to cross the sea; it would also open the way for durable solutions (repatriation, resettlement or local integration) in the region, without the refugees having to travel through numerous countries. Nonetheless, and in order to ensure that protection in the region is not going to be used by Europe as a substitute for offering asylum, such a policy needs to be coupled with a resettlement commitment from the member states so that asylum seekers are given the possibility of seeking protection in Europe as well. This is particularly important in cases of family reunion, vulnerable cases such as women and unaccompanied minors, or where protection in a certain transit country is not efficient or does not lead to a durable solution. The refugees' own preferences, plans and family ties would also need to be taken into account.

The concept of regional protection programmes is also not too far from the UNHCR approach, which advocates that solutions to refugee problems should be found first and foremost in the regions of origin and close to them. UNHCR has supported the concept of regional protection programmes as long as they are not seen as a substitute for protection in Europe, and has also suggested that the approach is more comprehensive, involving local actors in the areas of humanitarian aid, development and external relations (UNHCR, 2007b).

Considering that the asylum systems and legislation in many transit countries are weak or non-existent, pursuing such a policy would mean substantial capacity building work to: improve the states' capacity to process, receive and protect asylum-seekers; set up a registration scheme; provide support to local infrastructure (financial and operational support) and the legal framework; and assist refugees to gain their livelihoods and integrate in the transit country. Such programmes need to be protection-oriented and situation-specific. More importantly, they would need the full commitment and political will of the transit countries in order to work together, enhance their capacities and build an asylum space. This it not as evident as it might seem either. As we shall see in Chapter 5, some North African countries, for example, have been particularly reluctant to develop their asylum systems to protect refugees found in their territory, and this despite having signed the 1951 Geneva Convention.

A couple of 'regional protection programmes' have already started in the Western Newly Independent States (Ukraine) and the Great Lakes Region (Tanzania).[28] North Africa is another area where such a policy could also make sense. At the same time, work has already been done at a more preparatory level in order to support the capacity of certain countries in the area of asylum, particularly through projects with international organizations and refugee-assisting NGOs. UNHCR has been supported with B7-667 and AENEAS funding to carry out such projects in North Africa. The UNHCR project 'Institution building for asylum in North Africa' implemented in 2005–6 was a first attempt towards creating an asylum space and aimed to test the ground, collect essential background information and address pressing protection needs. In practice, this project tried to collect information on the situation of refugees and migrants transiting through North Africa, while supporting the capacities of the countries in the area of asylum, supporting the capacities and presence of UNHCR to ensure both delivery of protection wherever necessary (and while a state asylum system is still absent) and the empowerment of local civil society, whose work in this area has been important yet fragmented. The project was the very first step at a time when the situation of asylum seekers in countries like Morocco was particularly bad (see Chapter 5).[29] A follow-up project is now carried out by UNHCR in North Africa and some Middle Eastern countries, with funding from AENEAS.

These kinds of projects have received strong criticism from certain academic and activist circles, which see in them a Trojan horse for the 'externalization' of EU migration policy. Schuster, for example, sees a link between the UNHCR B7-667 project and the infamous (rejected) proposals for extraterritorial processing, mentioned earlier, 'because they are part of the same logic, in that the existence of asylum systems will make it possible to designate these countries as safe third countries of asylum, and hence return people from Europe' (2005a, p. 4). Others have also voiced similar concerns, using them as an argument against capacity building for asylum in third countries.

One needs to take a step back to examine this line of argument. If brought to their logical conclusion, such arguments eventually mean rejecting the possibility of providing protection to refugees found in third countries on the basis of a fear that this might be abused by Europe. Besides unwittingly defeating the point which should be to increase and effectively deliver refugee protection, these positions fail to recognize that the vast majority of refugees are indeed hosted in developing countries – not Europe. They shift the attention away from the problem, and put Europe at the centre of the argument. This arguably Eurocentric position also has the implication of undermining transit countries' responsibilities and obligations to provide protection in accordance with the relevant international conventions they have signed. The dichotomy between countries that have a responsibility towards refugees and those that do not have such a responsibility is not one that can be defended ethically and legally. Certainly, Europe could also contribute by providing further opportunities for resettlement and alternatives for cases that fail to receive adequate protection in the region. This, however, should not diminish in any way third countries' responsibility to provide adequate protection, and Europe's work to support and strengthen these countries' capacities to do so. Even more so if the number of persons in need of protection that find themselves stranded in the region is constantly increasing, as Chapter 5 in this book will show.

This chapter has presented the overall framework and rationale of EU policy on migration and asylum in Europe, as well as in its relations with neighbouring transit and origin countries. In many policy areas, member states have been settling on the lowest common denominator approach. The differences between member states' national policies still maintain great divergence, making some member states more attractive destinations than others. This divergence also creates or transfers 'burdens' from one member state to another, as the Dublin regulation illustrates. Asylum systems still differ in terms of reception conditions, recognition rates and administrative procedures. As a result, migrants may not apply for asylum in the first member state they enter but remain in transit, hoping to seek protection at a later stage. In that sense, the current EU asylum policy framework and its application is directly conducive to a strengthening of transit migration. The case of Greece, presented in the next chapter, is exactly about this phenomenon: Greek asylum policy is restrictive and inefficient, and refugees are discouraged from staying. At the same time, informal labour practices allow for migrants and refugees to survive in transit and this way, they end up staying in Greece for significant periods.

In the area of labour migration, EU policy is still lagging behind; there is a need for commitment in labour migration and the development of a framework for admissions. An admissions policy would prevent people from taking the illegal path, paying smugglers and risking their lives, and would give them the prospect of realistic employment opportunities in Europe. It would also provide migrants with a clear and specific destination, thereby undercutting one of the main factors creating transit migration. A structured framework for admissions and recruitment could substantially decrease the need to spend long periods in transit whilst undocumented. To the contrary, the EU seems to have done a lot of work to develop the control and prevention of illegal migration component, perhaps at the expense of an admissions policy, which is more difficult to agree between member states. A number of measures and operational support to the member states through FRONTEX are in place to ensure efficient border control. A framework for search and rescue operations is now also on the table. Nevertheless, the current approach to border management is not sensitive enough to the humanitarian and protection issues that arise with the mixed flows of people. Further work is needed in order to integrate a more protection-oriented approach in border management, namely that of ensuring access to asylum procedures to those in need.

The external dimension of EU migration and asylum policy has been developed further during the last couple of years, with a gradual mainstreaming of migration and asylum within the Union's foreign, economic and development policy with third countries. The 'Global

Approach to Migration' introduces a more comprehensive conceptualization of cooperation for migration management, putting it in a broader context. In fact, a comprehensive approach is the only way to reconcile the EU's concern to prevent irregular migration, the transit and origin countries' needs, and the need to provide legal migration channels, respect human rights and provide access to protection for refugees, all in one. As far as the neighbouring transit countries are concerned, cooperation in matters of migration and asylum is part of a partnership on various levels. As Lindstrom (2005) argues, the Union's Neighbourhood and Partnership Instrument may become an institutional outlet for creating a more normative framework for asylum and migration. A substantial part of the Union's partnerships with third countries consists in support for capacity building in migration and asylum. There has been controversy over the development of asylum in transit regions; nevertheless, the need for protection to be available in the regions is pressing, as the case study in Chapter 5 will illustrate. At the same time, this should be accompanied by an EU-level resettlement policy in order to fill in protection gaps and give sufficient guarantees that protection in the region is not used as a substitute for the possibility to seek asylum in Europe, should one need to.

The various strands of EU policy and objectives presented in this chapter may not always relate explicitly to transit migration. Yet they all have a major role to play in the evolution of the phenomenon, both inside and outside the European Union. These policies provide the essential background for understanding the case studies in the following chapters. Chapter 3 will turn to the case of Greece, a member state on the periphery of the Union that has been a destination country for a number of migrant groups, as well as a transit country mostly for refugees coming from the Middle East to Europe.

3
Transit in Europe: The Case of Greece

Bêrîcan

We didn't know anyone in Greece, or anywhere else for that matter. But if you want to find a *kaçakçi* ['smuggler' in Turkish], there are so many around it is very easy, and they give you information about where to go, what to do, everything. But you know what, they promise you that in Greece there will be accommodation in a reception centre and jobs and social benefits ... and there is nothing like that. We knew nothing, just rumours, and we came here and found out the truth.

The main problem is that when you arrive, and from the time you apply until you get recognized [as a refugee], you have no coverage. You get the 'police note' and for six months you are like nothing here, you cannot work legally, if they arrest you this paper is no protection. And then after the interview, they examine your case and let you know, maybe in another six months. So you are not covered for at least one or two years. In other countries they do this much faster. We thought we were coming to Europe, but this is very far from what we expected.

Yes, I have a refugee status now. It was a very tiring procedure. I applied, was rejected, made an appeal, was rejected, second appeal, in the end I got the refugee status. I applied in 1998 and got asylum in 2001. I had almost given up by that time. My brother came to Greece as well; he stayed two years waiting for his papers, and then at some point he was frustrated from waiting and decided to leave and he went to Sweden. He called me and said that his papers were done within a day, and that it was great there.

It's been some years in Athens now ... in the past we thought of leaving, to go to Sweden, or the UK or Canada. But now is too late.

We don't care about going elsewhere anymore, we are fine here, we have a place to stay, we have made friends ... This way or the other, we will earn a living. I don't think it will be any different in Sweden, in Holland or anywhere. I would do the same things and live this type of life anyway. And people will not be any better, I am sure. I really cannot start from scratch now.

It's just a matter of how you feel here, how much you care that the state does not give you anything, that things are so informal and you have to survive on your own. If you get used to that, you stay, if not, you go. And if you have started a life here, well, you stay.

You know, we had different plans, my husband and me ... I wanted to study, become something. Here I am nothing, and I will always be nothing. My husband was an artist back home, now he is nothing. He works in a sweatshop. But I wanted him to become something, be known. There is no present for us here, and there is no future. When you are a refugee, this is how it is, there is no present, no future, only past.

(Kurd, interview in Athens, January 2002)

3.1   Greece: destination and transit

Greece is usually not pictured as a migration hub in the international media, definitely not as much as Italy and Spain, which seem to monopolize all the attention in the Mediterranean. Some studies on the Mediterranean even fail to make a reference to the country at all. Nevertheless, the numbers of irregular migrants arriving in Greece are equally large. In the year 2007, Greece was the third most popular destination country for asylum seekers in the industrialized world with 14,700 applications, and received far more asylum seekers than any other Mediterranean or Western European country (UNHCR, 2007a).[1]

A number of reasons make Greece a popular destination and transit country. Geography is one of them. Positioned at the south-eastern end of Europe, Greece is a Schengen country sharing land borders with some of the migrant source countries (Turkey, Bulgaria, Albania). Greece has the longest coastline in Europe, about 16,000 km, which is almost three times that of Spain and slightly longer than that of China, and includes 3000 islands and islets. However, geographical reasons alone cannot explain the phenomenon. Greek migration policy does not give opportunities for long-term settlement, and asylum policy is extremely restrictive, making it almost impossible for refugees to receive effective protection. Greece has a vast and long-established informal economy that absorbs and sustains undocumented labour. A prevalent informality in structures and social networks creates an environment where semi-legality is tolerated and survival is possible. Repeated regularizations give the message that a residence permit is eventually a matter of time, for those that wait long enough. Furthermore, the lack of European public attention means less funding for migration management and refugee reception infrastructure. It also means growing reluctance on the side of the Greek state to deal with these migration flows on its own.

Over the years, Greece has developed into a popular destination for the Balkans and the Middle East. It is common to present Greece as a 'new' immigration country in Europe. One can wonder, however, for how long a receiving country can be described as 'new' (and 'unprepared'), considering that migrant communities now have a history of over 15 years in the country. Other Southern European countries that also became immigration countries in the 1990s have mostly abandoned this 'new immigration country' thesis. It seems that, in Greece, this argument is still used as an excuse to account for policy deficiencies. At the same time, society still sees migrants as temporary labour and has not come totally to grips with the migration reality. This is also reflected in the way migration and asylum policy has developed during the last ten years. This chapter will draw out the profile of Greece as a migration and asylum country, and analyse how transit migration was born and sustained throughout the years.

Greece has a long emigration history. The country saw almost one million of its nationals leaving for Western Europe, America and Australia between 1946 and 1977. The size of return migration has been equally large: by the mid-1980s almost half of the migrants to Northern Europe and three-quarters of political refugees had returned home. In addition, more than 200,000 ethnic Greeks from the former Soviet Union have been migrating to Greece, most in the 1990s, and many were granted Greek citizenship. Prior to that, another wave of ethnic Greeks had been the arrival of almost 1.5 million refugees from Asia Minor in the 1920s, following the Greek–Turkish war and the exchange of populations set by the Lausanne Treaty in 1923. With respect to the relative size of migration flows of all types (emigration, return, immigration), the Greek experience has been unique in post-war Europe (Fakiolas, 1999). Despite this turbulent migration history, the arrival of migrants in the last two decades has been experienced as a sudden phenomenon.

Today Greece has more immigrants in proportion to its population than any other Southern European country. According to the 2001 Census, there are 762,000 registered labour migrants in the country. The Census was carried out before the completion of the 2001 regularization programme. Taking this into account, as well as the registered refugees and asylum seekers, 'returnees' from the former Soviet Union, and irregular migrants, most estimations put the number close to one million (Cavounidis, 2002), in a country of 11 million. They originate from Eastern Europe, the Middle East, Asia and Africa. In particular, the largest groups are Albanian, Bulgarian, Romanian, Pakistani, Ukrainian, Polish, Georgian, Indian, Philippino, Moldovan, Russian, Bangladeshi, Iraqi, Nigerian. According to a 2001 survey, most migrants from the Balkans and Eastern Europe arrived in 1992–4 and 1996–8.[2] Migration from these countries has now stabilized and the communities are settled with jobs, social and cultural associations, newspapers and churches.[3] Most Africans and Asians arrived after 2000.

Greece has also been host to refugees, mostly from the Middle East (Iraq, Turkey, Iran, Afghanistan), Pakistan, Nigeria, Somalia and the former Soviet republics (Georgia, Russia). Many among the Middle Eastern refugees and asylum seekers were Kurds. Refugee flows peaked in the years 1989–90, 1996–7, 2005 and again in 2006–7. Greece continued receiving asylum applications even when the overall number dropped in Europe in 2003. The relatively small number of registered asylum seekers and refugees during the last ten years has given the impression that the refugee issue in Greece is minor. For the period 1990–2003 Greece received 47,030 asylum applications, having a share of 0.9 per cent of all asylum applications submitted in Europe.[4] By the end of 2006, the refugee population consisted of 2289 Convention refugees, 12,267 new applicants and 13,054 registered asylum seekers whose application was still pending. For the same year, Italy received 10,348 new applicants, and Spain 5297.[5]

One should also take into account that rejected asylum seekers (in fact 98 per cent of applicants are rejected) are more likely to remain in the country undocumented. In addition, a large proportion of refugees do not lodge an application in Greece at all, as they feel they have more chances of obtaining asylum elsewhere in Europe. All in all, the refugee population in need of protection may not be as small as initially thought.

Most migrants and refugees are employed in the service sector, agriculture, construction, tourism, domestic service and manufacturing, in jobs that natives usually do not take. A significant proportion of migrants working in agriculture come from neighbouring countries and are employed on a seasonal basis (Vaiou and Hadjimichalis, 1997). There is a predominance of women in the domestic service and care sector, particularly from the Philippines, Eastern Europe and former Soviet Republics. Trafficking and prostitution has also been on the rise, involving Eastern European but also African women, predominantly Nigerian.

Irregular migration is vast and estimates put the numbers in thousands, even though it is hard to know the exact number of undocumented at any given time. A recent government estimate put the number at 100,000 for the year 2006.[6] Collecting data is by nature difficult and estimations tend to rely on border apprehensions and arrests inside the country. To get an idea of the scale, 7994 people were arrested for illegal entry at Greek borders in 2005 and another 22,151 in 2006. In the first half of 2007 the number of irregular entries from Turkey reached 17,897.[7] Another common source is regularization data. These figures, however, may differ substantially. None of them can be taken as a basis for estimates; the number of border apprehensions does not record the 'successful' entries, nor the second and third attempts. Mobility between cities or across borders makes estimations even more difficult. Moreover, and contrary to public impressions, the vast majority of undocumented migrants do not enter the country illegally, but enter and then overstay their visas.

Migration and asylum policy

It is only recently that Greece started to develop a more adequate legislative framework for migration and asylum. Until 2001 migration was regulated by a 1991 law that was not responding to the migration reality as it evolved during the 1990s; Law 2910, introduced in 2001, was the first serious attempt to manage migration. An important step was the transfer of authority from the Ministry of Public Order (MPO) to the Ministry of Interior, signifying a change in the perception of migration as a home rather than security issue (Skordas, 2002). Border control, visas and asylum still remain a matter for the MPO today. The law set one-year renewable work and residence permits, and introduced a framework for seasonal recruitment through bilateral agreements. In addition, Greek consulates abroad were to have recruitment offices with job-matching services as a form of admission policy to meet the country's labour market needs. Law 2910 was accompanied by a regularization programme.

Law 2910 had some important shortcomings (Sitaropoulos, 2003). The short duration of residence and work permits did not allow substantial improvements in the migrants' daily life. The job-matching idea was highly unrealistic, if one takes into account Greek local practices of recruitment in sectors such as agriculture, construction or manufacturing. It would have required much more, namely an analysis of labour market needs, the setting up of a recruitment system and awareness-raising campaigns in origin countries, so that migrants could be informed about this possibility.

Following the change of government in 2004, the New Democracy government passed another migration law (3386) in August 2005. The law was more or less along the same lines as the previous one, keeping many of its provisions including the pending yet improbable consulate 'job-matching' function. A single document replaced residence and work permits, but their duration remained one–two years renewable and they were job, location and employer specific. A certain degree of deconcentration was proposed at administrative level. The law mainstreamed the EU Long-Term Residents and Family Reunification directives into Greek legislation, albeit in the most restrictive fashion.

Law 3386 did not manage to overcome long-standing problems, such as the duration of residence permits and the flexibility of work permits, especially considering that they would have to correspond to the needs of a flexible labour market predominant with informal, seasonal and ad hoc practices, as in the Greek case. The law opened the debate on integration, a major challenge in the years to come, without, however, giving any substance to the overall objectives. Migrants still rely almost exclusively on their own survival strategies, social networks and civil society support.

Regularization programs have been a core feature of Greek migration policy, regularly proclaimed as one-off solutions for the undocumented. They have followed a pattern of short permits, proof requirements that are hard to meet and administrative inefficiencies that create long queues, making the measure incomplete and bound to be repeated. Many migrants have been unable to apply, as they could not meet the requirements or the fee costs, or their employers were unwilling to adopt formal employment procedures.

The first regularization was introduced in 1997–8. Migrants with one-year stay in Greece and payment of social insurance contributions were eligible for temporary residence permits ('white card'), while a proper work and residence permit ('green card') would need further evidence; 371,641 migrants registered for the white card, two-thirds of which consequently received a green card (Cavounidis and Hatzaki, 1999). The second regularization programme in 2001 tried to cover those who did not manage to register with the first one, or did so but then fell back into irregularity. It was similar to the 1998 one, even though holding a work permit now became essential. The permits were valid for one year and renewable for a yearly fee. Another 351,110 migrants applied, many being applicants for a second time (Kasimis and Kassimi, 2004). Bureaucracy and poor staff resources created tremendous delays in the processing of applications. Applicants were granted temporary residence permits for two years until the backlog could be cleared. Many got trapped in an institutional gap between legality and illegality.

The 2006/7 Regularization programme was carried out in a similar fashion, and in fact was completed in two rounds, as the first one (early 2006) was too restrictive and bureaucratic to give the chance of registering to a sufficient number of applicants. It is estimated that the total number of residence permits issued by the government since its coming into power in 2004 and through these two phases of regularization was a quarter of a million.[8] In fact, the government seems to have turned regularizations into its main policy mechanism; the Interior minister announced in May 2007 that he aimed to use regularizations regularly and repeat them 'until no migrant remains illegal in the country'.[9]

Essentially, this regularization pattern shows a reluctance to give migrants the possibility to settle properly (Papadopoulou, 2005b), as they are not given sufficient time and opportunities to maintain and renew their legal status and build long-term plans. Many seem to swing from regular to irregular and back to regular status, or living with the constant anxiety whether their permit will be renewed this year or not.

The other major point on the Greek policy agenda has been the fight against irregular migration. Following the Seville Summit's emphasis on migration control, the Greeks were particularly keen to put migration on the agenda during their presidency in 2003; indeed, the Thessaloniki Summit highlighted the need for a common approach to irregular migration. They were not very vocal on asylum issues though. With an amendment to Law 2910 a set of measures were introduced in 2003 to fight smuggling and protect migrants found in the sea. The law sets stricter punishment, higher penalties and vessel confiscation for smugglers, and temporary residence permits and protection from deportation for smuggled migrants, until a decision on their case has been reached.

It is important to mention that Greek law gives undocumented migrants access to emergency health care and education for their children. Considering that a substantial proportion of migrants and refugees find themselves in some kind of irregularity while in Greece, this is an important benefit.

In the field of maritime control, the Ministry of Mercantile Marine has developed into a major actor, covering search and rescue and monitoring operations. Beyond national waters, Greece has been heralding its role in the management of sea borders and providing support to FRONTEX at EU level.[10] Greece would be particularly interested in support through joint EU operations for surveillance, and search and rescue at sea. Considering its long coastline and thousands of islands and islets, all of which are Schengen borders, the country has a strong interest in receiving assistance for the management of this maritime border

Cooperation with Turkey would be of primary importance given its geographical location as a favoured route. Turkey is a major transit country, equally reluctant as Greece to deal with migrants and refugees in its territory. Bilateral cooperation so far has been limited to a control mentality and no other strands seem to be further explored. The two countries signed a readmission agreement in November 2001. Few migrants are formally readmitted, however, as they usually lack documentation that can support a readmission claim. Turkey also seems reluctant to readmit migrants who passed through its territory, as it lacks readmission agreements with many countries of origin.[11] For example, out of 5600 applications that Greece presented to Turkey for readmission in 2002, only 100 were accepted at first instance and 34 after further negotiation.[12]

Similarly, between April 2005 and May 2007 Turkey accepted only 1646 illegal migrants from a total of 27,752 requests.[13] There is also no Turkey-EU readmission agreement yet that could generally back readmission claims from the EU side. On the other hand, the agreement also lacks safeguards for access to protection in Greece. On a number of occasions irregular migrants, including potential asylum seekers, have been sent back to Turkey by the Greek authorities while trying to enter the country, in this way prevented from even the possibility of exercising their right to seek asylum (Sitaropoulos, 2003). The quality of protection in Turkey is also a point of concern. Turkey has ratified the 1951 Geneva Convention with a geographical limitation to grant asylum only to refugees coming from Europe. In light of its EU candidacy, Turkey is bound to undertake reforms in the area of migration and asylum, including the lifting of this geographical limitation and the creation of reception infrastructure. Scholars fear that all these developments will shift the border eastwards and increase immigration to Turkey (Frantz, 2003; Kirişçi, 2003; Brewer and Yükseker, 2006). However, migration flows to Turkey seem to be part of broader processes, such as modernization, socioeconomic change and geographical location, and are most likely to continue in the future, irrespective of these reforms.

Greece has also signed readmission agreements with most neighbouring and some source countries, namely Albania, Bulgaria, Croatia, Bosnia-Herzegovina, Romania, Russia, Ukraine, Tunisia, Egypt, China and Pakistan.[14] At the same time, Greece is also known to have resorted to informal deportations. The history of police round-ups and mass expulsions of the undocumented goes back to the early 1990s, when 379,259 Albanians were deported in 1992 alone (Petrinioti, 1993, p. 17). Deporting torture victims and persons in need of special protection has also been reported by local and international organizations. NGOs argue that Greece has not ratified the Fourth Protocol to the Convention for the Protection of Human Rights and Fundamental Freedoms that prohibits (Article 4) mass deportations.

In the area of asylum, Greece is surprisingly restrictive. Asylum was established with Law 1991 and the 1996, 1998 and 1999 amendments. The MPO is the competent authority. The refugee status determination procedure is extremely long, between one and three years on average, and in 98 per cent of cases it is negative. Like Bêrîcan's story presented earlier, many applicants have to wait for years for an answer. Applicants are first given a 'police note' of registration until the examination of their case starts. This note may be the only administrative paper in their hands for some time, yet it does not hold any particular value in preventing deportation. Once registered as 'asylum seekers', they are given a temporary residence and work permit ('pink card') giving access to employment. Considering the lack of assistance and social care, this right to work is a particular advantage.

The recognition rates are extremely low: in 2006, the recognition rate was 0.6 per cent for refugee status for both first instance and appeal review decisions – 1.2 per cent if one also includes humanitarian status, which is most probably the lowest in Europe. In Italy, for example, it was 7.3 per cent (refugee status) and 44.5 per cent (including humanitarian status), in Spain 9.1 per cent (refugee status) and 18.6 per cent (humanitarian status), and in the United Kingdom 12.2 per cent and 23.3 per cent.[15] Certain applications are reportedly 'frozen' at an early or appeal stage, most of which are made by Iraqis, and this even at a time when Iraqi refugees in Europe are seen with added sensitivity (European Parliament, 2007). Asylum seekers are not informed about negative decisions in sufficient time so as to lodge an appeal. Access to asylum at harbours, airport zones and points of entry is difficult.

The reception infrastructure is poor and hardly in a position to meet refugee needs (Sitaropoulos and Skordas, 2004). Greece has ten reception centres, with the Lavrio camp being the oldest. The most recent one, in Kyprinos close to the Greek–Turkish border was opened in June 2007, and two more are to be opened soon on the island of Samos and in Chalkida, central Greece. Most reception centres in the islands of the Eastern Aegean, close to the Turkish coast, are more or less used for detention. Many more spaces are used occasionally as temporary reception areas. During my fieldwork in 2001–2 refugees were known to live in the reception camps in central Greece and around Athens (Penteli, Lavrio, Nea Makri and Elinas), and a few in reception halls in central Athens. In theory, migrants are only allowed to stay there for a few weeks or a couple of months. Nevertheless, in the camps I visited in Penteli and Lavrio there were cases 'stuck' for months or even years. Overcrowding is common and reception conditions are unsanitary, degrading, and at times inhuman. The camps usually lack specialized staff, including interpreters to inform the refugees about their rights and possibilities. In a visit to Samos in June 2007, the European Parliament LIBE Committee delegation found that those who do not lodge an application are released and given one month to leave the country. It is almost certain that most disperse in the country and continue to stay irregularly in Greece for some time. Similarly, migrants in Mytilini are initially kept in the reception centre for three weeks with the aim of being deported. As deportation or readmission to Turkey becomes impossible due to lack of documentation, migrants are released and asked to 'leave for any destination they prefer' within a fortnight (Lauth-Baccas, 2006). A similar situation has been observed in the Canaries, whereby migrants are transferred from the island reception centres to the mainland and released in order to leave the country within five days (European Parliament, 2006d). It has also been observed in Italy and in mainland Spain (Carling, 2007a). In the LIBE Committee's view, the reception centres in Greece show complete disregard for obligations established by the Reception and Procedures Directives.

Local authorities and government commonly argue that the poor infrastructure is due to lack of funds, as creating camps is at Greece's own expenses. It is true that the 'official' numbers of registered asylum seekers and refugees, which is the standard reference point for the allocation of funding from the European Refugee Fund (ERF), are too small to bring substantial funds to Greece: for the period 2000–4, Greece received 2 per cent of the ERF funds (or 2.7 million Euro), while Germany and Italy got 50 per cent.[16] Had there been proper registration of the beneficiary population, clearing of the backlog and a more generous asylum system, the data presented would be closer to reality and provide more funds. Most of the funding was for 'reception services', meaning care, maintenance and services provided by NGOs, rather than the building of reception infrastructure. It is a further question whether Greece has also been proactive in pursuing more funding for reception purposes. On the other hand, it is undeniable that in the context of undocumented mixed flows, handing out funds on the basis of 'official' numbers only sees part of the reality. Some other possibilities should be made available to share the 'burden' with the continent's gatekeepers, in the style of a burden-sharing approach discussed earlier.

Many migrants are taken directly to detention, and only if they express an interest in lodging an application are they transferred to reception centres. Detention is used as a standard practice and not as an exception, including detention of minors. Certain nationalities may be detained for months (European Parliament, 2007). Asylum seekers and migrants rarely have access to a lawyer or interpreter while in detention. Malta, for example, also displays similar practices in detention and reception conditions (European Parliament, 2006c). In general, asylum seekers in Greece often remain without any information about their rights or the procedures applicable and rarely have access to interpreters and legal aid.

The conditions described above do not provide sufficient guarantees for protection in Greece. As a result, many refugees do not apply for asylum in Greece and prefer to remain undocumented in order to have the right to apply later in another member state. This reflects the inadequacies of the Dublin regulation, explained in the previous chapter. It is striking that in a 2007 ECRE advocacy paper about the devastating effects of the Dublin system, the majority of cases that were presented had entered Europe through Greece; they had not applied for asylum while in Greece (ECRE, 2007). It is also worth noting that few Dublin regulation cases are presented to Greece from other countries, and even more rarely are they accepted by Greece (Papadimitriou and Papageorgiou, 2005) Others apply in Greece just to have access to employment and health care, but still leave for Western Europe. Transit has become a standard phase for forced migrants reaching Greece. Similar practices have been observed in Italy, with Kurds registering or even obtaining papers and then leaving for Germany (Schuster, 2005b). In a similar way, refugees arriving in Spain may not want to lodge an application, but remain undocumented in order to apply elsewhere in Europe (European Parliament, 2006d).

On the other hand, Greece also uses the transit argument as an escape to shift the 'burden' of reception to the 'traditional' destination countries. Ironically, the other countries are no different when it comes to finding a pretext to avoid refugee reception; just as Greece assumes that refugees are only temporarily staying in the country, and uses transit migration as a pretext for its neglect, Western European countries assume that asylum seekers will be rejected and returned home and use this as a pretext for their own lack of will (Zetter et al., 2002).

Public perceptions and the role of historical memory

As in most of Europe, the discourse on migration in Greece is a mixture of security concerns and recovery of ethnic identity. And as in most of Europe too, the EU is given a 'responsibility' role in the migration debate. The paradox, however, is that here security arguments coexist with a strong humanitarian discourse. The media discourse is rather emotional when it comes to boat people in distress, praising the locals' spontaneous assistance and criticizing the government for being negligent and incompetent. The humanist argument is picked up also by politicians, and humanism and hospitality are valued as integral to Greek culture:

> More and more arrive to Greece every day hoping to hide in a truck that will lead them to a country with better living conditions. What are they going to say about our Greece, that is the country of hospitality and democracy?[17]

As we shall see in Chapter 5, this hospitality argument is also employed in North Africa. Whether a cultural feature or a 'face saving' strategy, hospitality is present in the debate without, however, going as far as to compensate for policy gaps.

Similarly, the racism argument is often dismissed as happening elsewhere, in 'Western Europe'. The very strong sense of a differentiation between the 'Self' and the ethnic 'Other' – sometimes referred to as 'cultural racism' in the literature (Wren, 2001) – is not perceived as a form of racism. The historical circumstances in which the country was formed and evolved still has a significant impact on popular perceptions of minorities and mixed cultures, that differ in important ways from other European countries. Ethnic origin seems to be seen as the basis for membership (Triantafyllidou, 2000). 'Multiculturalism' is often employed in public debates to reaffirm modernization. Similarly, it is interesting to note that the discourse surrounding local initiatives to assist migrants reveal a motivation that is based on compassion and humanism rather than a strong conviction in the principle of rights.

Yet, as much sympathy as they show, one can safely assume that the public would not be ready to go so far as to endorse a more lenient or flexible migration policy. Humanism is advocated as long as migrants are seen as temporary guests.

Interestingly enough, while transit migration is common, there is no particular term in Greek to describe this phenomenon. It is usually referred to with phrases like *'those who don't want to stay here'*, *'those who are temporarily in/passing through Greece'*, focusing on a potential outcome. Transit migration is usually referred to as an uninteresting phenomenon about which there is *no need* for research or debate, precisely because of its provisional character. On the other hand, when referring to the country, the idea of Greece being a transit country does raise concerns.

Refugee flows are also seen as transient, justifying the need for aid but not for proper settlement. As a result, governments have never been very attentive to refugee needs. Refugees are seen with sympathy, and what is more, they are seen with solidarity. This relates to the Greek experience of 'refugeeness' (*'prosfyghia'* in Greek) and *'xenitia'* (which could be translated as 'the painful experience of living abroad, away from one's homeland'), both powerful notions in public ideology. Through the Lausanne Treaty (1923), which marked an end to the Greco-Turkish wars of 1919–22, a compulsory exchange of populations took place between Greece and Turkey, in order to 'enhance' the ethnic homogeneity of the territorially finalized states. The result was the resettlement of more than a million ethnic Greeks from Turkey to Greece and about 500,000 ethnic Turks from Greece to Turkey. The successful inclusion of this population was a landmark in Greek history that shaped the society, economy and culture in the following decades. 'Refugeeness', that is, the living memory of displacement, resettlement and rebuilding livelihoods in the host society, encompassed the first and second generation of refugees as a central identity feature (Hirschon, 1998). Considering that the Asia Minor refugees made up one-fourth of the total population of four million in the 1920s, a large part of today's population is of refugee origin. 'Refugeeness' is also alive in the second generation – seen as a hereditary element of Greek identity and valued as a term of honour (Voutira, 2003).

One would expect that with such a long migration and refugee history, the Greeks would extend this sympathy to migrants in general. Nevertheless, the memory of a migrant past is rarely employed to bridge the gap between 'us' and 'them'. On the contrary, only the refugee history is. Public discourse rigorously distinguishes between 'migrants' and 'refugees'. For the same reason, refugees are often referred to as '*political* refugees', to draw the lines of distinction more clearly.

The following example is a case in point of this solidarity. Established by Asia Minor refugees in the 1920s, Nea Smyrni is an Athenian middle-class borough where many locals have refugee origin. Even the name is a reference to the refugee past (Nea Smyrni: New Izmir). When Kurds – most of them undocumented and few with 'police notes' – arrived in the area and squatted abandoned houses back in 1999, the locals did not object but showed solidarity and support. They set up a 'Voluntary Committee in Support of the Kurdish refugees of Nea Smyrni', prepared weekly clothes and food donations, and even warned them of police checks and deportation. They extended their water and electricity supplies to provide to the squatted houses. Elderly residents in particular were most touched and 'opened their arms' to the newcomers, as I was told at an interview with the local council. At the same time, they all tried to lobby the authorities for proper resettlement in a refugee camp. Having to balance between a strong solidarity ideology and the rule of law, the local authorities eventually opted for 'benign' neglect.

What is more, like many of today's Kurds, it was Turkey that the ethnic-Greek refugees were fleeing from some 80 years ago. On the basis of this link, the Kurds have been welcomed by the Asia Minor descendants, and by Greeks in general, with a particular sense of solidarity. This Greek–Kurdish solidarity has been predominant in Greece in the late 1990s, and is related to Greek–Turkish relations and the perception of the Turkish 'Other'. It has also provided fertile ground for the accommodation of Kurdish Diaspora politics in Greece in the late 1990s. I observed in my interviews that the Kurds were aware of this Greek affinity, and from their side, they used this 'ascribed identity' as a basis for mobilization:

[When we came to Greece] we thought that you Greeks, because you have suffered from dictatorships and other wars and the Asia

> Minor catastrophe, you would understand us. You are the only
> country in Europe that can understand us and help us.
>
> (Kurd, interview in Athens, July 2002)

Solidarity apart, the fact that refugees also take an irregular path to
enter Greece, using the same boats and smugglers as the rest of
migrants, creates some confusion for the public. The public finds
it hard to distinguish between the refugees' *means* of travel and their
needs. This is also reflected in the way terms like 'economic migrants',
'irregular migrants' and 'economic refugees' are used interchangeably.
State officials and the public often share the impression that asylum
seekers are, in fact, labour migrants abusing the asylum system. This
may be true for some. For most, however, the problem lies in the fact
that it is hard if not impossible to present documentation as evidence
for their story. Many do not fit the Geneva Convention definition
of 'refugee' but may still need protection (e.g., victims of non-state
agents or generalized violence). This is most common among refugees
in various parts of the world, and solutions are often found through
complementary forms of protection.

The fact that many refugees live in transit or refuse to apply for
asylum until they reach another country only serves to complicate
matters and reinforce this suspicion, along with the reluctance to give
anything more than provisional solutions. The following section
vividly displays this temporary reception attitude; based on fieldwork
and unpublished archival material from NGOs, the story takes us back
to the mid-1990s when the first reception centres were created in
Greece to meet urgent refugee needs. This experience has marked the
way in which refugee reception is perceived in Greece today and in a
way, it has marked the very beginning of transit migration there.

3.2   A tale of refugee camps

It all started in the summer of 1996, when 700 Kurds from Iraq sud-
denly arrived in Athens and set up tents in a central Athenian square,
close to Omonoia, the very centre of the Greek capital. With local elections only a few weeks away, the issue immediately attracted attention.
The Athens local council tried to resettle them, and shortly before the
elections the Kurds were provisionally transferred to a state-run children's summer camp in Aghios Andreas, in the northern outskirts of
Athens. While not meant to be a camp, the place saw the population
mushroom in only a few months, reaching 1800 in November and

2500 in December 1996. In eight months, the camp hosted over 12,000 Kurds (from Iraq and Turkey) and Iraqi Arabs. Living conditions were appalling – overcrowding, lack of heating, food shortage, unsanitary standards.[18] The refugees set up a committee and organized hunger strikes and protests.[19] Lacking both the means and the will to cater for the refugees, the Athens local council soon handed over the issue to the government. The camp population survived the following year on NGO assistance and private donations.[20]

A crucial issue was the legal status of this population, as nobody had actually applied for asylum by that time. Since a case-by-case examination of 2500 people would be hard to achieve in a short time, it was proposed to collectively grant the Kurds temporary protection with a temporary permit that would also include a work permit. Asylum might be considered as an option at a later stage. Temporary residence permits were not new in Greek policy; it was the standard type of permit granted even to refugee status holders back in the early 1990s (Black, 1992). The temporary permit card fell short of the Kurds' expectations, who were hoping for refugee status. The authorities, on the contrary, were hoping to provide temporary relief but to prevent permanent settlement and discourage further arrivals. In the end, the Kurds had to take the offer.[21] Those who arrived in the following months, however, were refused temporary permit cards.

It soon became clear that a proper asylum system was needed. Act 2452/1996 on refugee issues was put forward in December 1996, but came into force two years later. Amongst other things, the new law regulated the status of temporary protection, provided for work permits and the setting up of reception centres.

Once this was sorted, the Ministry of Health and Welfare, in charge of the camp population, asked for evacuation. With no place to go, the refugees hardened their stance. They refused to go and lobbied for a proper refugee status determination procedure (RSD), financial assistance, protection against deportation, and asylum or resettlement in a third country.[22] The Ministry consequently turned to a different solution, proposing job placements around Greece. The refugee committee agreed on the condition that employment would be based on proper contracts and salaries, transportation to the region, accommodation and asylum. In the end, 208 refugees were transferred to Crete and 182 to other cities and recruited in seasonal work. The plan was not particularly successful: 95 per cent of the Kurds returned to Athens, 80 per cent of them after a week and an additional 15 per cent within two months.[23]

By spring 1997, after six months of the camp's function, the situation had not changed much. Most refugees either held a temporary permit card or remained in the camp hoping to obtain it; only 100 Kurds had actually applied for asylum. The refugees lobbied for asylum *and* resettlement. Refugee mobilization, now backed by Greek human rights groups and trade unions, became more politicized.[24] The Ministry of Education, owner of the camp, also joined in the debate and requested that the camp returns to its former use. The government was not only inexperienced in refugee reception, it also seemed to lack the will to find a solution. Threatened with expulsion, the refugees staged a hunger strike:[25]

> We decided to play the game. In order to put more pressure, we left some homeless in the street. When Greeks see singles [refugees] they stick to the letter of the law, but when they see families, well, something happens and they are very sensitive. And so they were touched.
> (Kurd, interview in Athens, October 2001)

The government agreed to start the RSD procedure and grant humanitarian status to those rejected; families would be resettled in proper accommodation, yet to be created. A promise was given to stop deportation orders, as *'a sign of the government's good will'*.[26] The authorities 'created' refugee camps overnight, converting public buildings and summer camps: 250 refugees were transferred to a children's summer camp in Sounio, south of Athens and 250 to an Agrotiki Bank-owned building in the holiday resort of Loutraki, close to the city of Corinth. The refugees remained in these camps for some time; a year later, in 1998, the Sounio camp population had doubled. Another 100 people, mostly families and pregnant women under humanitarian status were sent to a camp in Nea Makri, north of Athens.

During the next months and into 1998 two more reception camps of this sort were created, again close to Athens, in Aghios Stefanos and Penteli. Refugee flows to Greece also continued unabated. Starting with 600 people, the Penteli camp reached 1500 in January 1998.[27] The refugee committee, based in the Aghios Andreas camp and coordinating mobilization for all camps, again lobbied for resettlement using the same type of pressure:

> The government was confronting us again; the families had to leave the Nea Makri camp. So again, we pressed by leaving the families in the street. And then, about 25–30 families were given a place in

Penteli. That was a big success, I remember it was Sunday and yet we managed to get the government to agree.

(Kurd, interview in Athens, October 2001)

The closure of the main camp in Aghios Andreas was now imminent. The Kurds staged a sit-in protest outside the camp, threatening to return to the city and squat in Omonoia Square if proper measures were not taken. The situation in the camp mobilized even Diaspora organizations outside Greece; the Federation of Iranian refugees in Germany sent a fax asking Greece to protect the human rights of the Kurds in Athens.[28] The camp finally closed on 16 June 1997.[29]

In general, during these two years little progress was made for proper reception and the refugees were constantly moving between camps in the Greater Athens Area. According to the Refugee Committee's estimates, 99 per cent of those who wished to stay in Greece had no papers.[30] UNHCR was lobbying to renew their six-month temporary permit card in spring 1997, but this also seemed to stagnate. In his letter to Amnesty International in November 1998, the president of the Committee of Iraqi Refugees described the situation as follows. Greece hosted about 4300 Kurds from Iraq with more refugees arriving every month. Apart from the camp populations, about 1000 Kurds were also homeless in central Athens. Kurds lacked not only refugee status, but also access to legal aid and, often, to the asylum procedure while in detention. Summary deportations were common. In this context, most Kurds were reluctant to apply for asylum in Greece and hoped to leave for another EU country. Were the chances of obtaining asylum higher, or the reception and welfare standards more promising, they would prefer to stay. Indeed, few people tried to renew the temporary permit cards in 1997 – many had already left the country.[31]

Koummoundourou Square

Following this camp adventure, some Kurds still moved back to central Athens in July 1998 and created a settlement made of cardboard boxes in the neighbourhood of Koummoundourou Square in the very centre of town, next to the Athens Town Hall. By the end of the year, they had already reached 1500. NGOs, the church and locals were providing help to get through the winter. The square became a nodal point for drug trafficking and male prostitution, both of which benefited from the refugees' despair.[32] Unsanitary conditions and illnesses soon created an alarming situation for locals and refugees alike, which escalated when two Kurds died of hepatitis in February 1999. Civil society, refugees and political parties jointly advocated for a solution. The issue was repeatedly raised in Parliament. Finally, on the morning of 15 February 1999 the Kurds of Koummoundourou Square were woken up by the police, who, following a ministerial order, transferred them to the western Athenian suburb of Aghia Varvara, aiming to temporarily resettle them in a hospital. The locals of Aghia Varvara, however, reacted strongly to this unexpected arrival. Local authorities and the police spent hours negotiating outside the hospital, and the Kurds were eventually taken to a remote and run-down former American base in Mountain Pateras, west of Athens.

To the surprise of the police and the NGOs, the refugees refused to accept this resettlement plan. The next morning, only 23 Kurds were found in the base, out of the 350 brought in the previous night. The rest had left and returned to the city centre. This time they scattered in the city, fearing that if they settled as a group they might be removed again; some moved to the neighbourhood of Asyrmatos, others settled in run-down places or cheap hotels. Finally, the remaining 23 were transferred from the American base to the Nea Makri camp.[33] In response to the failure and heavy criticism of this operation, the government stated that local reactions in Aghia Varvara could not be foreseen, and that they were not aware of the conditions in Mountain Pateras.[34] Once again, the issue was not solved through proper measures but through the Kurds' dispersal in the city.

The operation was actually undertaken on the very same day of the arrest of the PKK leader Abdullah Öcalan (15 February 1999). The Kurdish leader had been on the run from Turkey, and no country seemed to be ready to take him in (the Netherlands even refused to allow the plane carrying him to land). On that day the world woke to discover that Öcalan had been apprehended by Turkish commandos as he was leaving the Greek embassy in Kenya where he had been secretly hiding. The arrest of Öcalan sparked off reactions among the Kurds all over Europe, from hunger strikes and self-immolations, to protest rallies and attacks on Greek embassies; 120 Kurds were arrested in Greece on that day.[35] The refugees were certain that the 'resettlement' operation was linked to Öcalan's arrest:

> It is because of the arrest [of Öcalan] that they were removed, because the atmosphere was very negative towards the Kurds and

the government was afraid that a group gathered in the city could be a cause for trouble.

> (Kurd, interview in Athens, December 2001)

The government denied any connection, claiming it to be coincidental.[36] Either way, it was clear that this episode would bring the first chapter of Kurdish refugee reception in Greece to a close.

Asyrmatos

The sequel of the story was played out in another Athenian neighbourhood, Asyrmatos, located between the three municipalities of Aghios Dimitrios, Dafni and Nea Smyrni. In spring 1999, about 200 Kurds started gathering and gradually created a settlement with containers placed in an empty lot. Despite the appalling conditions and the fact that the lot was literally next to houses, playgrounds and schools, this settlement lasted for more than a year. Again, it was the NGOs and locals that helped them survive. A 'Greek-Kurdish Support Committee' was formed and mobilized to move them to a proper settlement.[37] The three affected local councils tried to shift the responsibility to the government. It was only in February 2000, just before local elections, that the issue appeared on their agenda. Negotiations between the authorities and the Committee lasted for a number of months, until the police were finally sent to 'clear' the area in June 2000. As in Koummoundourou Square, the Kurds were again forced to leave; they scattered in the broader area and found shelter in run-down houses in Nea Smyrni, in the community described earlier in this chapter. This community remained and gradually increased in the following years; about 650–700 Kurds were living in the three municipalities in 2002, when I visited them.[38]

Patras

Patras, the western port of Greece, is the other big city where transit migrants have been concentrating with the hope of being able to stowaway in the ferries going to Italy. Irregular migrants have been gathering there since 1995. In the winter of 1997 around 300 Kurds moved from Athens to Patras and sheltered in containers and abandoned train wagons close to the port. As the number increased in the following months, the need for the creation of a refugee camp became pressing. After a hunger strike staged in January 1998, they were provisionally transferred to the Loutraki camp. With no permanent solution in sight, the refugees protested again, and, a few days later, they returned to Patras on foot. Others had reportedly left Patras with fake Swedish passports.[39] The Kurds stayed in Patras for a few years; a population of 2000 was living there up to 2002, lobbying the local authorities to *both* resettle them in third countries *and* improve living conditions in Patras.[40] Today the Kurds have been replaced by Afghanis and other nationalities, staying in Patras with the same prospect – to find a way out. In the first half of 2007, the coast guard confiscated 700 fake travel documents, 70 cars and 118 trucks carrying irregular migrants.[41] Some have applied for asylum in order to have the right to work and get health care. Similar practices have also been observed in Cherbourg, France, in 2007, where migrants have been living in a makeshift camp by the port and trying to smuggle themselves to the United Kingdom hiding on freight lorries.[42]

Debating refugee reception

Only a few months after the Kurds' arrival in 1996 the question of their reception was already raised in parliament. The pressing needs were accommodation, medical care and legal status. Admittedly unprepared for this phenomenon, the government held the reception offered as generous and sufficient. The government's main fear was that creating proper reception infrastructure would act as a pull factor. The temporary camps had 'unluckily' created hyperbolic expectations among refugees that they could find permanent accommodation in Greece. What is more, the refugees' 'transit' condition was a factor suggesting that there was no need for a reception policy:

> For these people that are here on the move, there is no way of monitoring. *This is not a population for which one can organize and implement programs and medical care.*[43]
>
> (emphasis added)

On two occasions, in Omonoia in 1996 and in Asyrmatos in 1999, resettlement was undertaken mainly in view of forthcoming elections. In addition, the estimated 24,000 Kurds living in Greece in 1997/8 were seen as 'irregular migrants of economic character'. The temporary protection that was granted in 1996 was perceived as an act of generosity:

We gave them a six-month residence permit even if they never asked for asylum. We still thought that we *could temporarily characterize them as refugees.*[44]

(emphasis added)

In other words, temporary protection was not seen as an emergency solution due to the difficulty of proceeding with a case-by-case examination, but as a substitute for residence permits granted *en masse*. This perception was in line with the overall approach in the 1980s and early 1990s, which was to ensure that Greece would not be a country of 'permanent' settlement for refugees, but of temporary asylum for refugees in transit (Black, 1994). The granting of work permits to temporary permit holders at this stage might strike one as odd, yet it was rather pragmatic considering that one way or another the Kurds would seek employment in the informal economy.

On the other hand, one has to acknowledge that the law amendment to create an asylum procedure was a sign of progress. The two year delay in its coming into force, however, prevented any improvement taking place during the time the problems were imminent.

It is striking that refugees became quite political in their mobilization and had substantial bargaining power. This was not the first time refugees had claimed their rights: in a similar way, 60 Kurds from Turkey were given work permits on a one-off basis in the 1980s after they had fought a political campaign (Black, 1994). The Kurds were consistent in their demands, yet their agenda often included contradictory items, such as asylum and reception *and* resettlement in a third country. To a large extent, refugee demands were shaped according to prospects; for example, when the plan for job placements was proposed, the refugees took the chance to lobby for proper employment. Assistance for resettlement in a third country was proposed when the government position was no more forthcoming.

The refugees' leverage drew both from the state's inexperience in how to cope with refugees, as well as from public support and local activism that built a 'support structure'. Locals were often running ahead of, or confronting, state measures. Local objections stemmed less from xenophobia, and more from concerns about the quality of life in the area for both the Greeks and the homeless refugees – in most cases, the areas chosen were underdeveloped and already suffering from a number of problems. The government was only trying to catch up with the events.

The stories presented above describe the origins of Greek refugee policy back in the late 1990s. The repeated pattern of refugee makeshift settlement in the centre, then relocation outside the city, and finally individual return and dispersal in the centre shows that the state was not willing to provide proper reception; instead, the solution was to make the population 'invisible', by letting the refugees disperse – and stay, knowingly, as undocumented in transit. This attitude and policy approach of provisional solutions has pre-marked the years to come and has created the conditions for transit to become a standard migration pattern.

The next chapter will focus in detail on the living conditions and experience of being in transit, as narrated by many of the people who went through the adventures presented above. This is complemented by interviews with newcomers, whose experience in 2001 and 2002 was very similar. The experience of being in transit, from the journey and the crossing of the borders to the arrival in Greece, and the way of life is not unique to this particular case; the risks, feelings, challenges and vulnerabilities are similar in North Africa, Eastern Europe and other regions where migrants spend part of their life in waiting.

4
Being in Transit

Sîwan

I came here because there is no way you go to another country without going to Greece first. That's all I knew about Greece before.

... I crossed the border to Turkey together with 50 others, went to Ankara and then to Istanbul. I stayed there for eight months, first in a friend's place in Aksaray and then elsewhere. I worked here and there. In the evenings I would go to a café where other Kurds were gathering. Sometimes people spoke about Greece, about how to get there, about the river and the mines [at the border].

At some point this guy said that he could arrange [the trip] for me, because he had a friend who was a soldier at the border checks, and he would talk to him. I could go and spend some time there and investigate the area, and then see how I could cross to the other side. The guy would pick me up and take me to the border. I thought that I have got nothing to lose, and so I went. The weather was good; it was August of 1998. He came and picked me up and brought me about 1 km far from the border, and said 'Now go, good luck!' I didn't cross right away, I stayed and hung out in the area for a week or so. Then I found a pass, I swam and crossed the river to the other side. I am a good swimmer, so I was not worried. When I arrived, I was still not sure I was in Greece. They had told me that if I walk in a certain direction I would find the railway lines and then I would find a street. And so I did. I found the railway lines, but when I got to the street I hid behind a bush and watched the cars. Only when I saw that the car signs were in Greek was I certain that I am in Greece. I was in the area close to Ferres. I hitchhiked, but nobody stopped. I was wet and I looked horrible. Finally, a gipsy stopped and picked me up, and I told him in half-Turkish half-English that I want to go to the nearest police station. And he brought me there. I got a 'police note' from them and then I went to Athens.

In Athens, I went to stay with a friend I found in Omonoia, he was renting a flat with five others. His job was selling tea: he was making tea at home, putting it in big pots and selling it in cups at the square, to migrants and passers-by. He was about to leave for Europe, so I took over the job and also took his place in the house. I did this job for 6–7 months, and it was good, I could make 6000 drachmas [€17–18] per day. The rent was not high, say 10,000 drachmas [€28] per head, so I could manage. But you can't do this job forever, so I gave up. Then I found an NGO that gave me some information and I came to live here [in the camp]. Sometimes I find a job here in the area, construction, gardening, this sort of thing … It's OK, I manage.

I save the money I earn, here in the camp I don't have that many expenses. I have sent money to a friend in Germany a few times: once he needed $500 to pay off a debt, another time his wife was giving birth and he needed money. I sent him. I know that if I am ever in need, he will also send me money. I also send money to my mother at home too. She is old … We speak on the phone sometimes; no need to go to a phone booth, I have a mobile.

When I don't have a job I hang out here in the camp. Sometimes I get mad hanging around like that, doing nothing.

… I am not a friend with everyone here in the camp, you want to have your own people, you know, the people you trust, and I only trust those from Iraq … I do not know about Kurdish parties in Greece, and I don't care. I don't like them, particularly the PKK.

I don't want to stay here, I want to go to Europe, that's why I never applied for asylum, or any other paper. I am illegal for three years now. I have tried to leave four times to go to Sweden. First time I crossed the border and went to Albania in order to go to Italy; the person arranged by the *kaçakçi* was there and picked me up, he put me in a truck but I was caught only a few kilometres further out, in the first town. Second time I didn't even get through the border. Third time I tried it another way, I went to Patras and hid in a ship, but was caught again, before the ship even departed. Fourth time I went to the airport, but was caught again. I wanted to go to Sweden because I have friends there and they told me that it is good. I don't mean in terms of jobs, I mean in terms of asylum policy, the papers and the benefits you get.

In Greece it is much better for work; honestly, I can find a job, any job, in a week. But you don't have any protection here. This time I am going to Germany, I have bought a ticket to Paris and friends will come and pick me up. I don't know which city we are going to. I am not afraid – if they catch me on the way, well, tough luck. I don't care, I've got nothing to lose. I have already bought a fake passport for Germany. Sweden was too expensive, the passport was $3000, Germany was cheaper. That was very easy, I just called up this guy we know and he got me one.

(Kurd, interview at the Penteli refugee camp, November 2001)

Sîwan's story is a typical case of a refugee in transit who is waiting for the opportunity to settle properly in another country. His journey is also one many others have when crossing from the Middle East to Europe on foot. In this chapter I will describe the phenomenon of transit migration as experienced by the migrants themselves. I will examine the organization of the journey and the smuggling business, the arrival and living conditions in transit and the feelings, hopes and difficulties migrants face during this phase of waiting. I will pay particular attention to the factors that shape decision-making, including factors that are often omitted in the literature for being non-quantifiable. Transit stories are similar, whether in Athens, Rabat or Moscow, and most of the observations made in this chapter could easily apply elsewhere.

4.1   The journey and the smuggling business

It is estimated that between 30 per cent and 80 per cent of illegal entries into Europe are 'facilitated' by smugglers.[1] One in three smuggled migrants is intercepted; the other two get away. Refugees also rely on smugglers to seek asylum in Europe. Increase in smuggling is a result of the absence of legal entry channels. Stricter border enforcement has boosted migrant reliance on smugglers, and as Spener (2001) rightly argues, it has increased both the fees and the potential for abuse.

Most of the people I interviewed had entered the country illegally. Half of them used a smuggler and the rest tried to smuggle themselves through the border. Only four came to Greece with valid documents, two with a study visa, one with a tourist visa and one in order to be reunited with her husband who was granted refugee status. It depends more or less on the budget. The poorest try to cross the borders on their own; smuggling services or fake documents might be equivalent to a years' salary. Still, it is important to note that those reaching Greece are not the poorest of all. In fact the poorest often do not even make it to Greece and remain 'stuck' in transit countries in the Middle East, Asia or Africa.

Before I present the smuggling practices for the crossing from Turkey to Greece, it is worth saying a few words about the nature of human smuggling in general and its implications. The media tend to attribute smuggling to ruthless criminal gangs who rule over international borders and waters. The public also seems to confuse smuggling with trafficking, and uses the terms interchangeably even though they are quite different types of activities.[2]

First of all, there is a different purpose and a different relation between the smuggler and the migrant than between the trafficker and the migrant, which essentially stems from the fact that the migrant has given his or her consent. With some exceptions, the migrant is aware of, and has agreed to, the particular action before leaving. Smuggling is often seen as a 'necessary evil' by the migrants rather than exploitation. One of the Kurds said to me that 'they are doing their job otherwise we would not be here.' A similar observation was also made by van Liempt and Doomernik (2006) in their research with smuggled migrants in the Netherlands, and by Bilger and colleagues (2006) in their research in Austria. It would be no exaggeration to argue that in some cases refugees even see smugglers as lifesavers that offer a way out of the country. This point also helps distinguish between means and motivation (Crisp, 1999), and prevents diminishing morally the person's claim to refugee status for illegal entry. Having said that, it remains undeniable that migrants are vulnerable at the hands of smugglers and cases of abuse are very frequent. Migrants are abandoned in the high seas, tricked and guided to a different destination, or they are stripped of their money, passports and belongings. Brewer and Yükseker (2006) report that Africans trying to cross from Turkey to Greece are often abandoned off the Turkish coast.

Smuggling is also organized differently. Trafficking is a job of mafia-style criminal gangs that often relate to drug trafficking, document fraud, money laundering, arms smuggling and other such activities. Smuggling is entangled with these sort of activities in some regions, for example in Afghanistan, in Southeast Asia or in Algeria, as we will see in the next chapter. Elsewhere, however, and at least in this Mediterranean border, smuggling is a small-scale action, with few people involved, of a casual character with no further dimension. Migrants may, in fact, hire numerous and different smugglers for each leg of the trip. The Kurds I interviewed used between two and three smugglers to cover the distance from their home town to Athens. Fickenauer (2001) and other scholars argue that smuggling can be better described as a crime that is organized rather than as organized crime per se.[3] In fact, organized crime has a number of additional defining attributes that are not necessarily shared by a smuggling network, such as, for example, a hierarchical structure, self-identification of the group, violence and a reputation for violence, etc. (Fickenauer, 2001). Smuggling activities carrying migrants are usually occasional operations. The networks may be small or large groups, have a few 'managers', 'contacts' and 'drivers', and they stand to make profit out of the 'migration business' as Salt and Stein (1997) put it. But they are not mafias of the scale, sort and mechanisms like those involved in smuggling weapons or money laundering.

Yet, trafficking and smuggling may and do overlap, as migrants might be first smuggled through the border but then fall into the trafficking business, as observed for example in Mali or Algeria.[4] Migrants may also be trapped into dept bondage, or become subject to physical abuse:

> There were also some who had arrived but not paid all the money, and they worked and gave money to the smuggler until the debt was paid. For these people the situation is not good, they are beaten up or tortured sometimes. I haven't seen torture myself, but I have seen people being threatened.
>
> (Kurd, interview in Penteli, November 2001)

Taking a broader approach, Andreas (2001) sees human smuggling as a spectrum of activities ranging from 'self-smuggling' to local level 'individual smuggling entrepreneurs' to 'transnational networks'. Bilger and colleagues (2006) present a similar analysis in the case of smuggling to Austria. The case study presented in this chapter includes mostly self-smuggling and individual entrepreneurs. In North Africa, however, smuggling may require networks of different scale. That could explain how, for example, Asian migrants from Sri Lanka ended up in Morocco on their way to Europe.

States usually do not consider smuggling as a human rights issue but as a crime against public order; the priority focus is shifted from the protection of the migrant to the protection of the state. Policies to combat smuggling are almost exclusively focused on law enforcement and border protection. Trafficked victims are more likely to receive a rights-oriented reception, whereas smuggled migrants are likely to face immediate arrest, detention and deportation without necessarily any consideration of their rights and vulnerability. Nevertheless, a number of issues raise concerns in terms of human rights protection, even when the smuggled migrants safely reach their destination. A large proportion of smuggled migrants are refugees. These should not be punished for illegal entry, but provided access to asylum procedures first. The UN Smuggling Protocol foresees that obligations of states under international law, such as the 1951 Geneva Convention in particular, shall be respected. All migrants have the right to claim asylum and the destination country has, under international law, the obligation of non-refoulement. In addition, the rights of migrants attempting illegal entry should be protected from physical abuse at the hands of smugglers or border officials. The Smuggling Protocol includes a number of provisions to protect the rights of smuggled migrants and prevent exploitation.[5] The Protocol also foresees that migrants are not to become liable to criminal prosecution for the fact of having been smuggled in (Article 5). It is not certain whether this actually prevents a state from prosecuting a smuggled migrant for violation of national immigration laws; it may vary according to the way in which the Protocol is incorporated into domestic legislation.

Those hiding in ships would not fall under the category of 'smuggled' but into that of 'stowaways'. Due to the ignorance of the carrier, they are usually omitted from the literature on smuggling and trafficking (Morrison and Crosland, 2001). Nevertheless, the category is very relevant to the case study presented here, as many are those that tend to stowaway in and out of Greece. According to the International Maritime Organization (IMO), a stowaway is a migrant who:

> at any port or place in the vicinity thereof, secretes himself [or herself] aboard a ship without the consent of the ship owner or the Master or any other person in charge of the ship and who is on board after the ship has left the port or place.[6]

In 1996, a set of guidelines were presented by IMO and endorsed on the allocation of responsibilities relating to stowaway cases. These guidelines were consequently introduced as standards and recommended practices to the Convention on Facilitation of International Maritime Traffic (FAL Convention) through amendments in 2002. The guidelines advocate close cooperation between ship-owners and port authorities, and return of stowaways to the country they embarked or their country of origin. The guidelines also state that stowaway asylum seekers should be treated in compliance with international protection principles. Nevertheless, it seems that disembarking stowaways from ships to a particular port is not always easy to resolve, and what is more, it does not protect refugees from the risk of refoulement.[7] As IMO's regular update on stowaway incidents displays, repatriation of Afghan, Iraqi and Palestinian stowaways were common in Greece in 2007 (IMO, 2007).

From the Middle East to Europe

The migration routes from the Middle East to Europe usually pass through Turkey. Another route, albeit less common, has been from Lebanon and Egypt by boat to Italy, Greece or Cyprus. A third, more expensive option has been to migrate to Jordan and from there, either to take the boat from the ports of Syria and Lebanon, or the plane to a European country (Chatelard, 2002).

Leaving Iran, the usual route is to pass by Lake Urmia close to the Iraqi–Turkish border. It is worth noting that up to recently Iranians were not required a visa to enter Turkey. Some Kurds from Iraq would also cross to Iran first in order to enter Turkey. When I carried out the interviews (before the 2003 war in Iraq), the route from Iraq to the Turkish border was relatively easy. Contacting smugglers in Baghdad and most towns of the North was also simple. They were known in the local community, some Kurds claimed that they had even seen advertisements in the local papers. My informants obtained fake (Iraqi and foreign) passports of all kinds from local vendors in Arbil, Suleimaniya and Kirkuk, who also arranged for the drivers and the trip to the border. Their job is similar to that of the 'tramitador' (facilitator) in Mexico, who provides 'coyotes' (drivers) and 'safe houses' for Mexicans going to the United States (Kyle and Dale, 2001). For passports and visas, the fee was usually paid in advance; in other cases, it was to be paid after 'successful' arrival. The fee is financed by personal savings and free loans from relatives and friends at home or in Europe. Prices range from $4000–$6000 to continental Europe, $8000 to the United Kingdom, $12,000 to Australia and $15,000 to the United States. For the journey from Iraq, Iran and Turkey to Greece, the price at the time of my interviews was between $1800 and $3000 depending on the type of crossing and use of smugglers. İçduygu and Toktas (2002), who conducted research on smuggling to Turkey around the same time, gave similar prices. Antonopoulos interviewed smugglers, smuggled migrants and the police in Greece in 2002 and cites similar prices, around $2000 for the crossing from Turkey to Greece (Antonopoulos and Winterdyk, 2006). A part of the smuggling fee goes for the bribes to border officials. Smugglers also provide information and guidelines about where to go and how to respond to border officials. They also affect the choice of destination of those without family/social ties in destination countries (Koser, 2001, van Liempt and Doomernik, 2006). Indeed, nine of the people I interviewed came to Greece, following the smuggler's advice.

In reality, few migrants can afford such a cost. As a result, the journey tends to last longer, even for years, as migrants stay in the transit countries to work and save money. As a result it is common that the Kurds, when asked, would break down the cost and the time for the trip in parts for example Iraq–Turkey $1000, Turkey–Greece $1000, Greece–United Kingdom $2000–$4000.

Once in Turkey, Van, Agri, Hakkari and other border cities in south-eastern Turkey are the usual concentration points. Some migrants registered with the UNHCR in Van and Silopi as mandate refugees, hoping for resettlement in third countries. None of my informants, however, had registered with UNHCR there, since they were hoping to come to Greece. From there they spread to the Turkish mainland going westwards. Istanbul is a nodal point in the migration route. It is hard to say how many irregular migrants live in Istanbul today. Danis (2006) estimates anything between 150,000 and one million. Aksaray, Laleli, Beyazit, Kumkapi, Yenikapi, Kücük Pazar are some of the boroughs where my informants stayed. Migrants would gather there to socialize, find work or get in touch with smugglers, known by the term 'organizations'. They might stay in 'safe houses' or in friends' places and survive on day jobs, from selling tea like Sîwan, to construction or other types of menial work. Fifteen among the Kurds I spoke to had spent between two weeks and a year in Istanbul.

In research on the other side of the border, Danis (2006) presents similar findings; Middle Eastern migrants arrive in Istanbul and remain undocumented, looking for smugglers to cross to Greece. Lately, migrants from North Africa have also been taking the rather unorthodox route via Turkey to reach Europe. An important factor has been that up to 2006, Tunisians, Moroccans and Algerians had visa-free entry to Turkey. As a result, many would take the plane and arrive as tourists. Others took the Syrian land route. Compared to the Middle Eastern migrants, they seem to spend more time in Turkey before making the attempt to cross. Once they have put some money aside, they will try to cross to Greece or take a boat to Italy. Suitcase trade between Turkey and the home countries is a popular source of income for the Maghrebi. Others work in sweatshops or construction; Moroccan women commonly work as nannies in Istanbul.

In addition, there is a growing African migration through Turkey to Greece. Brewer and Yükseker (2006) estimate that 4000–6000 irregular Africans lived in Istanbul in 2006. The numbers increase in the winter, and drop in the summer months when they cross to Greece. Turkish visa regulations for Africans were also liberal until recently. Sub-Saharan nationalities could easily obtain 15-day visas for business, recruitment by sports clubs or tourism in Turkey. As a result, many Sub-Saharans entered Turkey legally – by plane – and overstayed their visas. East Africans also took the land route and entered the country via Syria. There is also the case of African suitcase traders, particularly Nigerian, Senegalese and Ghanaians, who travel regularly in and out of Turkey, like the Maghrebi traders. At the beginning of 2005, however, the Turkish visa regime changed for most sub-Saharan African nationalities, limiting the possibilities of legal entry.

İçduygu and Toktas (2002) argue that smuggling is organized by networks of localities, with a series of drivers/middlemen/helpers involved throughout the journey. My informants also used various local smugglers/drivers for each part of the trip, all of which they referred to with the Turkish word *kaçakçi*, also used by Bêrîcan and Sîwan. The business is quite widespread: 1157 smugglers were arrested in Turkey in 2002 (İçduygu, 2004). Many are arrested annually on the Greek side of the border. Smugglers may be of various nationalities, including locals and foreigners. Migrants may also participate in the smuggling business for some cash. One Kurd was offered a job from a Greek smuggler with a deal to get half of the earnings:

> They wanted me, because I knew the passages. Imagine, if you bring ten Pakistanis, each paying $1500–$2000, this makes a total of $15,000–$20,000 per route. I thought about it a lot, in the end I said no, I am not going to sell my honour and do smuggling of people. On the other hand, I could do at least one time and have some cash to get started. I know some who did. Anyways, it's better this way, with a decent job.
>
> (Kurd, interview in Athens, December 2001)

Over the border

There are two main ways to Greece, by land through the Greek–Turkish border, and by sea. The Greek–Turkish border is a short strip of land marked by the River Evros. Half of the Kurds I met had to cross this river to come to Greece. The *kaçakçi* usually takes them to the border with guidelines for paths to follow (like the 'pateras' in the

Mexican case, Spener, 2001), and sometimes he accompanies them to the other side. They may have a specific contact waiting in a 'safe house' in Greece or may be left to find their way to Athens. Between the start of 2007 and September of that year it is estimated that 4532 illegal immigrants were arrested at the border, together with 97 smugglers.[8] Antonopoulos and Winterdyk (2006) also cite prices for the trip inside Greece, from the Greek–Turkish border to Athens or Patras.

However, not all migrants can finance the cost of a second smuggler to reach Greece and try to cross the river on their own, like Sîwan. A quarter of my informants crossed the border this way. A Kurdish woman from Arbil walked all the way from Iraq to Turkey and through the river to the Greek side while being three months pregnant. They do not always succeed the first time: one Kurd spent a year trying to cross and succeeded only on the seventh attempt. Every time, he would be apprehended and sent back before reaching the police station on the Greek side. One of the main risks in this operation is the minefield in the border area that is badly signposted and has cost the lives of 64 migrants in the last decade.[9] O'Brien (2003) argues that there are theories that some migrants are sent to follow the paths through the mines so that the Turkish army can trace the 'live' minefields. This point was also made by one of my informants. However, there does not seem to be any conclusive evidence to that effect, and accidents are more likely to be attributed to bad luck and the fact that migrants usually travel during the night. In fact, a very small percentage of people crossing the border end up on the minefields (O'Brien, 2003). Greece signed the Mine Ban Treaty of Ottawa in 1997, ratified in Parliament in 2002 (L.2999/2002). Turkey also adhered to the Treaty in 2003. Yet, accidents seem to continue in the border zone. Seven people died in Evros in 2005 (Landmine Monitor Report, 2006).

The Aegean

It is equally popular, particularly in the summer months, to cross from the Turkish coast to the Greek islands in the Eastern Aegean, some of which are tantalizingly close. According to the UNHCR, close to 4500 migrants have been intercepted or saved in the Aegean Sea since the beginning of 2007.[10] Departing boats now avoid coastal cities like Izmir, Canakkale, Bodrum, Cesme or Ayvalik and opt for more remote beaches along the coast. Half of my informants took the sea route and most were washed off to an island, and only a few to the Greek mainland. Back in 1997–8 it was estimated that a boat was leaving every other day.[11] The numbers may be smaller today, but the flow continues unabated.

There are different types of vessels for different budgets. A small plastic or other boat with engine costs $300–$400. Smugglers are usually on a different boat and accompany the migrants up to Greek territorial waters; they rarely come on board with them. A plastic boat without engine is cheaper, around $100–$150. Two of my informants hired a boat without an engine and crossed, the first from Cesme to Chios and the second from Kas to Kastellorizo. The cheapest option is a plastic, inflatable boat that migrants can row with their hands. In certain areas the distance between the two coasts is only a few miles stretch, and migrants swim their way through.

Distances are small but the Aegean Sea is rough and the crossing has cost numerous lives: 364 migrants drowned and another 369 disappeared in the period 1998–2007.[12] Most arrive exhausted and dehydrated.

As mentioned in the previous chapter, in some islands migrants may be provisionally hosted in a reception centre. They are often released on the condition that they leave the country soon. But once out of the camp, most just take the first ferry to Athens. Lauth-Baccas (2006) reports that in order to prevent overcrowding in the camp, the local authorities in the island of Mytilini have even paid migrants their ferry ticket.

Finally, migrants also hide in cargo ships, usually heading for destinations further than Greece. As mentioned, this was particularly common in Patras in the late 1990s. In 1999 a fire in 'Superfast Ferry III' brought the issue to the forefront: the bodies of ten suffocated Kurds were found in the ferry garage. In 1999 alone, the Patras coastguard arrested 1000 stowaways. It is reported that 2000 crossed over to Italy in 1997–9.[13] The issue has caused a fury in the local community, which was particularly concerned about the impact this could have on the transport business. The smuggling business was thriving with Kurdish and Afghani smugglers competing for monopoly. There were even clashes between the port authorities and smugglers from the two ethnic groups.[14] According to interviews Kurdish political groups were also involved in the smuggling business, organizing the flight of their party members to and through Greece. There have been reports that Kurdish parties (namely PKK/ERNK) also exercised pressure on smugglers to obtain control and a share of the profit in exchange for 'protection', pressure that resulted in aggressions and 'disappearances'. The ERNK spokesman in Athens denied any involvement.[15]

Destinations

Most of my informants came to Greece because it was the first European country they entered when leaving the Middle East, accessible even on foot, and because it is a safe country. Essentially their aim was to reach 'Europe', perceived as an idealized broad space of safety, protection and opportunities.[16] Greece was also offering the possibility to survive on day jobs in the informal economy.

A small proportion came to Greece because of existing family or social contacts. Those had already been given a detailed account of reception facilities and life in Athens before even reaching the Greek shores, from others who had recently done the same journey:

> We knew, even before we left how things are in Greece. We knew that there is no place to stay, that the laws will not cover you, that you will have to leave soon. Friends were telling us that they sleep in containers, they said 'don't make the same mistake we made'. We know very well. Greece is in Europe, but is not Europe. And yet we came.
>
> (Kurd, interview in Athens, July 2002)

Migrants tended to prefer personal contacts and word of mouth information rather than media information. Yet, one-third of the Kurds I spoke to arrived in Greece randomly and without prior information, and like Bêrîcan earlier, they were completely unprepared. They also had no particular preference as to the country of destination.

Contrary to dominant perceptions, less than half of my informants saw Greece as a passage to Western Europe. Those who did, wanted to join relatives or friends in other destination countries; or they were under the impression – based on rumours and hearsay – that certain countries have more generous asylum policies and efficient administrations. The United Kingdom, Sweden, Germany and France were the most popular destinations among the Kurds, followed by Canada, Switzerland, the Netherlands and Australia. Koser and Gilbert (2006) who conducted research in the United Kingdom argue that this information is usually misleading and that migrants and refugees arrive in the United Kingdom with high hopes. Similarly, Kaytaz (2006) describes how migrants came to Turkey based on rumours that crossing to Europe is easy, only to find out later that it is much more difficult. Inaccurate information increases frustration, vulnerability and the chances that migrants will remain in transit and undocumented for a while. Irrespective of the reasons that bring them to Greece, migrants very often change their initial plans. In fact, the majority (70 per cent) of the Kurds I interviewed would eventually prefer to stay in Greece should the chances for asylum and settlement become more promising.

4.2   What is it like being in transit?

How are these first months experienced in the transit country? What does it actually mean to be 'in transit'? How long do migrants live in transit, and when and how do they take the decision to settle or move on? These are some the questions this section will address.

Migration literature often fails to see the vulnerability predominant in transit migration. The first months after arrival are times of extreme poverty, hunger and harsh living conditions. The transit condition is rarely seen from a rights perspective, even though migrants find themselves in a particularly precarious situation. Their fundamental rights are not safeguarded and access to protection is frequently compromised. The following section describes the situation of surviving in transit in the Greek capital.

Living conditions

After a while spent in reception (or detention) centres, migrants make their way to the city. As described in the previous chapter, many of them may not leave the country but remain in Greece for some time, as undocumented or as registered asylum seekers. Most will sooner or later head for the large cities, and the majority end up in the Greek capital. They seek shelter in cheap hotels or at friends' places, in middle- and working-class neighbourhoods with Greek or mixed population. They usually have to rely on their own efforts and contacts for assistance.

The camps I visited hosted 'police note' holders and registered asylum seekers. Some of them had been there for years. They were housed in old buildings and sheds in appalling conditions. Overcrowding was common. It was hard, even for the social workers, to monitor migrant mobility in and out of the camp. The rooms and sheds often lacked basic facilities, like heating and running water, and it was difficult to maintain proper hygiene. Toilets and kitchens were shared Tand the refugees took shifts in performing household tasks. The rooms I visited had only beds and a few personal belongings – family photos, a Sura from the Koran on the wall, a radio, children's toys, clothes.

Women and children usually stayed in the camp and men worked in day jobs in the area. Every morning they would gather in certain meeting points in town, where locals would pick up workers for the day. As a Kurd, a father of two, commented, 'if we get a job twice a week, we are really lucky.' Otherwise, they would spend their time watching Kurdish satellite television in the camp, or frequent the cafes in town. Women did not work; I met only one widow that worked in a restaurant in the village nearby. Life in the camps was reclusive and the contacts with the outside world rare.

Socialization was usually developed around ties of ethnic origin, language and political affiliation. In particular, ties of common town/area of origin were quite strong and bound by reciprocity and solidarity, similar to kin (Faist, 2000). However, friendships in the camp were usually temporary and often ended when leaving the camp.

Outside the camps, the Kurds would rent flats in neighbourhoods of Greek or mixed population. Singles that could not afford the rent would move in together with others, four or five people in a flat. Contacts with Greeks substantially facilitated relations and negotiations with the landlord. The poorest and the undocumented would often seek shelter in run-down houses. They lived in poor conditions, often lacking electricity, toilet and running water. Nonetheless, such settlements sometimes lasted for years. The Kurdish community of Nea Smyrni (Chapter 3) lived there for over three years, despite all the hardships. They worked in construction and other jobs, and sent most of their savings to their families back home. A satellite dish was perhaps the only 'investment' during their stay in this neighbourhood. Living undocumented means a lot of hiding. The Kurds would frequent only certain areas they felt safe and avoid neighbourhoods they didn't know. They also changed houses frequently to avoid being caught. Despite all this, three years later, the majority of this group wanted to stay in Greece rather than leave for another European country.[17]

Stay, or move on?

How does one take the decision to stay in the transit country or move on? Migration research usually cites formal or quantifiable factors, such as the role of receiving policies, resources, family and social networks, the progress of the asylum application, or the type and duration of residence permits. Indeed, all of these factors are significant. For persons in need of protection, the possibility of being granted asylum or not is obviously crucial. Kurds who had been granted refugee status were not interested in migrating to another country; similarly, about half of the asylum seekers and 'police note' holders that I interviewed stayed in Greece hoping to be granted asylum. For the rest of migrants, the possibility to obtain a residence and work permit is an important reason to stay.

On the other hand, some would stay in the country long after their application for asylum had been rejected. This was also observed in Turkey by Brewer and Yükseker (2006). There are a number of other factors, social, economic or personal, that may be equally important in decision-making, but are rarely mentioned as factors affecting migration. As common sense as they may sound, they are usually neglected because they are not quantifiable, predictable or directly implicated with policy-making. Having a job that pays reasonably is an important reason to stay, irrespective of status; the prospect of greater job stability, even through informal arrangements, makes it even more noteworthy. The prospect of proper housing in the present or near future is also a vital motive in this direction. Speaking the language plays a role in the decision to stay or continue to another country. Leaving will depend also on savings and the possibility to finance another trip. Often the money that is earned in the transit country is hardly enough to meet daily needs. Besides, most migrants, including asylum seekers or the undocumented, send money to their relatives at home. It takes a year or two in order to be in a position to pay off debts and put some money aside. Another factor is pride and social pressure from home to 'succeed' in the migration venture, especially if other family members depend on this migration: 'there is no way back now; I've come all this way. What will they say?' confessed a young Kurd. It is worth noting how migrants would avoid admitting failure or disappointment to their family back home. Two of my informants explained how they tended to present their life in Greece as a success and exaggerate, if need be, the accounts of their lives.

On the other hand, even if a second journey is possible, the migrant may be in poor health, feel tired or simply lack the energy to go through this process again. Some Kurds, like Bêrîcan in the previous chapter, felt that they had started a life in Greece and were not willing to move to another country. It may also be frustration, depression and a general feeling of distress as a result of leaving, losing family, home or friends at sea. All migrant stories are accounts of tragic events, loss, memory and true suffering. Even the least tragic migrant stories are accompanied by loneliness and stress. It takes substantial energy to pursue this kind of venture, and many are not willing to go further. Fear is an additional factor: fear of being caught on the way, fear of losing one's life, fear of the unknown. An important reason to stay in the transit country is feeling safe and comfortable with the place and its people. The Kurds and other Middle Eastern migrants mentioned feeling comfortable in Greece and found many affinities with Greek society, mentality and culture that helped them integrate rapidly. To this, one should also add the refugee history and solidarity ideology described in the previous chapter. On the other hand, many did not feel the same for Western European or Scandinavian countries. Korac (2001) observed a similar case with former Yugoslav refugees in Italy. On the contrary, we will see in Chapter 6 that Russia feels unwelcome, uncomfortable and unsafe to many groups of transit migrants, and for this reason they are keen to leave the country as soon as possible.

All these factors take shape in the transit country. This phase is used as a reservoir of resources and a hunting of opportunities that in the end determine the course a migrant's trajectory will take. The length of transit stay does not seem to make a difference: some Kurds stayed in Greece contrary to their initial plans, while others, who had hoped to settle in Greece, decided to leave after two or more years. A few Kurds had been to other countries, but then returned to Greece because they found less prosperous conditions for settlement. Finally, return to the home country was rarely mentioned. Only two people (from Iran and Syria) wished to return in the near future.

Networks

Family and social networks play an instrumental role in transit migration and deserve particular attention. The various functions and roles of social networks have been well accounted in migration literature. Boyd (1989) analyses the multiple ways in which networks support the migration process. Massey and colleagues (1993) explain how social networks can continue a migration flow, increasing the likelihood of those who stayed behind to join their compatriots aboard. They also make particular reference to ties based on the common village ('paisanaje') and ties of voluntary associations in Mexican migration that bind migrants through solidarity, common origin and common purpose. Koser (1997) applies a social networks framework to the analysis of the asylum cycle. Faist (2000) analyses the meso-level of social and symbolic ties and the use of social capital as a 'local asset' and a 'transmission belt' in migration.

All these show that networks are active throughout the migration process, starting from the organization of the journey. Crossing the border from homeland to Turkey is usually assisted by family networks (Danis, 2006). Friends in Turkey or outside are also the ones to provide the financial and, sometimes, organizational support for the journey to Greece (Shepherd, 2006).

Furthermore, life in the transit country would not be sustainable if it were not for the social ties that make survival and settlement possible, and in a way, foster a first level of integration. Migrants mobilize whatever social capital they have available at this stage from extended friendships, to ethnic ties or ties of common town or region of origin, common language or political affinities. More important are the social ties with locals, from the employer who provides a form of 'protection', to the NGOs, associations and local civil society that make up for policy inefficiencies. Ties with the host society are a true social capital and an important source of information, assistance and advice – a true 'support structure' for migrants. It was clear that those among my Kurdish interviewees who integrated most easily and rapidly were those with good Greek contacts. A similar phenomenon is also observed in the case of other migrants groups in Greece, such as the Albanians (Hatziprokopiou, 2003).

Danis (2006) observes that in Turkey this first-level informal integration is incomplete, precarious and contingent on policies. It is also fractional, as migrants integrate in certain niches of society in relation to the social capital they mobilize. This could also be observed in other countries, where migrants share some of the characteristics with the host country, such as common language, or religion or common ethnic origin, and the migrant population is stratified along these lines. In Greece it may be less fractional in the sense that transit and settled migrants, asylum seekers and refugees alike are absorbed in the broad pool of low-cost foreign labour. There are no linguistic, religious or ethnic ties with the host society which African or Asian migrants could build on. There is, however, a niche that Kurds in particular found in Greece, namely political mobilization, as we shall see further below.

Beyond local friends and compatriots, transit migrants rely substantially on family and social ties across borders as a means of survival (Chatelard, 2002). Especially in the first months after arrival, transit migrants seem more concentrated on the maintenance of ties at home and in other countries, than in the place they are staying. Many among the people interviewed in the camps were not interested in socializing in the camp, and even less with locals and Kurds outside the camp, and knew very little about the city and Greek society. Instead, they kept regular phone contact with their friends in Germany, Sweden and England. Transnational networks offer a sphere of communication and a reference point to a social group that spans borders. Whereas they could not visit their homeland, some informants travelled (legally or illegally) to visit friends and get an idea of reception conditions in other destination countries. A Kurd from Turkey spent the first year in Greece, then moved to Switzerland for a year, returned to Greece for four years, then moved again with friends to Germany and stayed there for another four years and finally returned to Greece in 2001. In all these stages he followed the track of ties in each country, which also helped him find jobs and supported him financially.

In a study on Salvadorians in the United States, Bailey and colleagues (2002) observed a similar situation, which they called 'permanent temporariness', where migrants remained in a prolonged status of temporary protection and employed survival strategies that were operating across borders. Transnational ties were sometime invisible, as they involved less physical and material movements and more intangible connection across borders through information, communication and feelings.

Nevertheless, as Koser (1997) observes in the case of Iranians in the Netherlands, the relation to networks is also shifting during the asylum cycle. Thus, once the conditions for permanent settlement become more prosperous, transnational networking loses its intensive character.

Waiting

The transitional period can be prolonged and uncertain. Life in the camps is quite isolated and cast in a constant expectation for change. They are all waiting: for money to come from abroad; for the examination of their asylum case; for a steady job that would allow them to move into a flat. It is often what comes first that will indicate whether they stay in Greece or not. For the unemployed, especially women and teenagers, this situation can be very stressful:

> I don't know what to do here; I wake up at 5am, eat, then sleep again, then wake up and do the house and then nothing. I am lucky there are the girls next door and we spend time together. But still, I can't stay at home like that. It's freaking me out …
>
> (Kurd, interview in Penteli, October 2001)

It is a situation of living 'neither here nor there', of being somehow 'in-between'. This was exactly the feeling and situation of the Kurds in the refugee camps: uncertainty, anxiety, the condition of being in-between places and phases. Being an asylum seeker or 'police note' holder in a refugee camp was an administrative category, but not a condition with which they could identify. Instead, they would rather identify with a community whose members were either back home or in other destination countries. They were hoping to see this phase end soon and lead to settlement and normal life:[18]

> You know, back home we had a nice house with a garden and a normal life, we had everything; and now here we are in the camp, living like the pigs ... And they call us 'asylum seekers' and 'illegal migrants'. I don't know about these names, I don't feel like one. I only know that I want to leave this place as soon as possible and start a normal life, like everybody else; in Greece or in England, where my brother lives. That's what I am waiting for, a normal life.
>
> (Kurd, interview in Penteli, October 2001)

In other words, being 'in transit' is a process rather than a status. Its outcome will depend on whether conditions, such as those described previously, change so as to allow for proper settlement. What is marking the shift from transit to settlement is when the conditions improve and the migrant feels that living and working in the country is stabilized, and, essentially, when uncertainty and insecurity fade. Some of my informants had evidently passed the transit phase and focused their attention on how to rebuild their lives in the medium and long term in the host society.

Being in transit is a vulnerable condition in various ways. Transnational networking does not relieve migrants of their daily problems. Transit migrants are an invisible population living in the margins, with no obligations, no rights and only partial legal protection. Undocumented migrants and rejected asylum seekers live with a constant fear of being arrested and detained or deported. 'Police note' holders may be technically registered, but not protected from deportation. They all have the right of access to emergency health care and education for their children, yet these are easily compromised for migrants who have not secured a proper resident status, or do not have good Greek contacts. Transit migrants, especially those in the camps, suffer from various health problems, physical and psychological strains. NGO efforts can only meet the needs of a small number of migrants. They are in a dire financial situation; occasional day jobs can hardly meet individual and family needs. Hunger and poverty are common, particularly among the undocumented.

In short, poverty, semi-protection, unemployment and social exclusion are the main characteristics of life 'in transit', fostering a process of marginalization rather than integration. The first couple of years in a host country are a precious time for establishing ties and access to resources, familiarising oneself with the authorities and the local culture and finding a niche in the labour market. Instead, this time is wasted and migrants are pushed to the margins of social strata. Nevertheless, though transit migrants may be vulnerable, they are not passive and helpless. They are active agents who try to set down a foot in the country and work for their future.

Politics in exile: the 'organized'

A particularity among the Kurds in Greece and other host countries has been their division between 'ordinary' refugees/migrants and the 'organized', Kurds engaged in homeland political organizations abroad (see also Griffiths, 2002). Interestingly, Danis (2006) found a similar distinction between politicized and non-politicized Kurds from Iraq living in Turkey. The first were not particularly keen to migrate to another country, whereas the latter would try to cross to Europe as quickly as possible. It is worth saying a few words about this 'partisan' migration, because these Kurds were indeed in transit, yet with a different purpose and under different conditions, and they have also been received differently by the host country.

The 'organized' Kurds came to Greece because of their party. Their migration was also organized through channels that the party had been using to secure its members in exile.[19] The groups in Greece were part of a transnational network of members and representations in various countries, whose main purpose and scope was to internationalize the Kurdish national issue. The ERNK office in Athens served as 'Representation for the Balkans';[20] the magazine *O Agonas* (the struggle) was the Greek version of *Özgürlük* published in Austria, Belgium, France and the United Kingdom. Compared to Germany, the United Kingdom or Sweden, their size and scope of activities in Greece was rather small (a few hundred people according to the interviews). They were active mostly in awareness raising campaigns and social/cultural events targeting the Greek public. Unlike groups in other European countries, the parties in Greece did not engage in activities directed to the construction of national symbols, identities and practices for the Kurdish community resident in the country. In addition, a parallel of Greek–Kurdish associations and Greek leftist groups have been backing Kurdish political mobilization. A turbulent history of bilateral relations between Greece and Turkey has nurtured a negative perception of the Turkish 'Other' and provided a particularly fertile ground for Kurdish mobilization. In other words, Kurdish political activism was tolerated in Greece because of its agenda as political, and not as migrant activism.

The 'organized' defined their experience in relation to the party and the political project. Five among my informants came to Greece because of their association with a certain political group and, what is more, in order to contribute to this group's international work. They would stay in Greece 'as long as it was requested by the party'. The journey, arrival and settlement of the 'organized' in Greece was taken care of by political networks. Some stayed in refugee camps, others were picked up at the border and transported to 'party' houses in Athens. The presence of politicians in the refugee camps was quite limited, even though there have been rumours about political activism in the Lavrio camp, south of Athens. While being temporarily resident in Greece, they did not seem to share the same migration trajectory with those 'in transit'. They did not face the same anxiety, uncertainty and vulnerability. In fact, the 'organized' remained focused on their cause, and on the side, they would do part-time jobs and socialize with Greeks of certain political affinity.

On the other hand, Kurdish political organizations showed a remarkable lack of interest in refugee/migration issues and the problems of ordinary refugees in Greece. In the United Kingdom, Kurdish politicians have worked together and through the Kurdish Community Centres to provide services to the refugees. In this way, the politicization of associations and their orientation towards the homeland has been a useful resource to refugees (Wahlbeck, 1998). Similarly, in Germany, immigrant and homeland politics overlapped and reinforced each other, in a way that 'foreign policy becomes integration policy, and integration policy becomes foreign policy' (Ostergaard-Nielsen, 2000). On the contrary, in Greece the 'organized' tended to distinguish themselves from the 'illegal migrants', as they called the non-politicized newcomers. They saw themselves as different, as exiles dedicated to a 'noble' cause rather than to a simple effort to rebuild their livelihoods.

The failure to develop a community-wide refugee agenda was also due to internal political rivalries and disputes transported from the home countries over to Greece, which generated resentment among the non-politicized Kurds. On their side, the non-politicized also preferred to remain distanced from Kurdish politics as they failed to represent their needs, at least not without exchange:

> They said 'give us money' and if you said no, well, they would say that you are a traitor ... If they know you, it is safer for you to pay them.
>
> (Kurd, interview in Athens, December 2001)

The Öcalan arrest in February 1999 made visible the risks that a Greek–Kurdish 'solidarity' strategy could have on bilateral relations with Turkey. Moreover, the event had an adverse effect on the Kurdish refugee population and its reception in general, irrespective of whether they had been involved in Diaspora politics or not. In fact, the incident had an impact even on Kurds from Iraq and Iran, who, in theory, were dissociated from the Greece–Turkey equation. As a result, Kurds – particularly the newcomers – tried to distance themselves as much as possible from politics. When I carried out the interviews in 2001/2, only a few Kurds admitted having a political affiliation during our first meeting. The political groups based in Greece had also decreased in size, and their activity had also lost some of its outreach. It is likely that many 'organized' Kurds returned home to Turkey in the next years, even though it seems more probable that they moved to Germany, France or the United Kingdom.

This chapter has focused on the transit experience as narrated by the migrants themselves. Organizing the journey, finding smugglers and crossing borders – land or sea – is a multi-stage process with many stops on the way and time spent in various cities. Despite the hard living conditions, migrants tend to stay in the transit country for some time. And contrary to dominant impressions, few migrants have specific plans before leaving their homeland. A number of factors and circumstances in the transit country will determine the course of the particular migrant trajectory. Living in transit is a state of being neither here nor there. Refugees are the most vulnerable among those in transit, as access to or delivery of protection is easily compromised. Finally, the chapter concluded by presenting a particular aspect in the history of Kurdish refugees in Greece, their mobilization in homeland politics. While also transient, the migration of the Kurdish activists remained quite distant from the transit migration of the mainstream both in terms of purpose and organization. The next chapter takes us outside European borders to the neighbouring North African region that in recent years has developed into an exceptional migration hub.

5
Transit in the Maghreb: Sub-Saharans and *el-harga*

5.1   Migration trends and policies in North Africa

According to the MPI, there are seven to eight million irregular African migrants living in the EU today. Two-thirds of these are estimated to be from North Africa, particularly Morocco, Tunisia and Algeria. Migration flows from Africa to Europe have increased substantially during recent years, and almost all of them take the irregular path. The issue has attracted substantial media attention. However, much of the impact of these migrations is not in Europe, but in the transit countries.

North Africa is a passage for all Africans trying to reach Europe. All characteristics of 'transit' migration identified previously are also present here. As far as motivations are concerned, migration flows are mixed, including refugees in need of protection and migrants seeking a better life. The majority are men, even though many more women are now making the trip, single or with children. Some of the women and children are 'passive migrants' or what one could potentially call the side-effect of migration flows – spouses or children that travel along with the head of the family, but then due to an unlucky incident, are stranded and left on their own. Unable to go back, they are bound to continue the journey wherever the particular flow of irregular migration is taking them.

Just as observed in Greece, most migrants want to go to Europe without however having a particular destination in mind, and fewer are those that migrate in order to join family and friends in a certain country. In addition, some may not be interested in going to Europe at all, and would rather stay in the transit country. Smuggling is also organized in the form of small and medium networks. Nevertheless, as distances are bigger, the trips costlier and the control infrastructure weaker, and as most of the population in the region is poverty-stricken, it is very common to see smugglers involved in other types of criminal activities as well, like trafficking for prostitution or forced labour or drug smuggling. Migrants also find themselves involved or trapped in these activities when they start the long journey to Europe.

Simon (2006) estimates that between 100,000–120,000 sub-Saharan Africans reach the Maghreb annually out of which only 20,000–35,000 actually cross to Europe. To this, one has to add the migrants that manage to enter Europe legally. Nevertheless, in total, the number that stays in North Africa is higher than the one that manages to cross. In fact, many get 'stuck' in the region for some time. Transit migrants, as we have seen, typically survive on day jobs and in certain countries, like Libya, the labour market seems to provide many informal opportunities for low-cost labour. Transit migrants in North Africa face the same situation of extreme vulnerability and uncertainty, human rights abuses and the constant risk of arrest and detention.

As far as the countries are concerned, they seem rather reluctant and completely unprepared to host migrants and refugees who happen to be in their territory. Facing a number of important economic and social development challenges internally, their main preoccupation is to avoid becoming destination countries for other nationalities as well. As a result, they commonly attribute the cause of transit migration to the neighbouring European Union, whose 'closed doors' policy can only but shift the burden to its Southern neighbours. At the same time, they are also very keen to seek financial and technical assistance from Europe as they are unable to deal with the problem alone. Moreover, the transit countries of North Africa are particularly unwilling to engage in asylum issues, sharing the same suspicion observed in Greece that asylum is an alternative migration path – this way undermining the asylum system and the international refugee protection regime. They are also particularly concerned about their international image, which proves to be a major factor mobilizing cooperation with Europe. As in Greece, hospitality is also valued as integral in local culture and often evoked in public discourse.

What makes things more complicated in this part of the world is that more than half of the transit migrants are not nationals of third countries, but the region's own children. Indeed, contrary to dominant impressions, sub-Saharan Africans make up only one-third of the migrants crossing to Europe. In fact, the number of Maghrebi migrants in Europe is much higher than the number of migrants from western Africa, with the Moroccans being by far the largest community (de Haas,

2007). Even minors emigrate for Europe unaccompanied (Baba, 2006). It is striking that the Maghrebi attempting to cross the sea to Europe ('el harga' or 'harraga' as they are commonly called in Algeria and Tunisia, literally meaning the 'burned'/ burning') are not necessarily the poorest or least educated. Morocco, Tunisia and Algeria, in particular, show great concern about this irregular emigration of their own nationals. This is also reflected in the way migration is debated with European counterparts. Asking for visa facilitation, for example, is the most common request in exchange for cooperation in border control and migration management. It is interesting that when one uses the word 'migrants' in Tunisia or Algeria, the locals' first reading of the word is of compatriots living aboard. The transit migrants are usually referred to as 'Africains', 'subsahariens' or 'clandestins'.

Hence, there are two types of transit migrants in North Africa: sub-Saharan Africans travelling through North Africa with the hope of crossing to Europe, and Tunisians, Moroccans and Algerians leaving either from their own country, or moving to the neighbouring country in order to cross to Europe. All Maghrebi have had visa-free entry to the other Maghreb countries since the 1960s, as per the Treaty establishing the Arab Maghreb Union (Article 2). This also provides the right to employment (after giving priority to country nationals). In addition, Tunisia also has bilateral agreements on seasonal work with Libya (1965) and Algeria (1966), allowing free circulation in a border zone of 15 km on each side of the border. Nevertheless, migrants may move and stay in the other countries as undocumented.

What creates and sustains transit migration in North Africa? It is true that the push factors in Africa, from conflict, violence and ethnic strife, to hunger and poverty, are as pressing as they were ten or fifteen years ago. Yet, it is only recently that transit migration of this scale made its appearance in the Maghreb. The Sahara and Sahel regions are traditional spaces of trade and movement of people across the continent. Migration paths follow the steps of past routes across the desert. Nevertheless, development in infrastructure, telecommunications and transport has made migration easier. New roads, mobile phones and money transfer now make it possible to coordinate groups of people and organize the smuggling across borders; information is circulating more broadly and people hear from others about the possibilitities of migrating further north.

A recent history of independence in North Africa and regional disparities in terms of growth and development between the north and south of the Sahara make the Maghreb more appealing. The African north is safer, politically more stable and economically more open. Moreover, refugees fleeing conflict in Africa do not find the necessary safeguards for protection in the Maghreb and as a result, they remain in transit. There is also a history of sub-Saharan African migration for study purposes, especially to Morocco and Tunisia, that now seems intertwined with transit migration. A similar phenomenon is observed in the former Soviet republics. Evidently, restrictive migration policies in Europe only contribute to migrants being pushed to the periphery. In other words, rather than being a mere epiphenomenon of European restrictive policies, migration through North Africa is part of broader structural changes in the region (Bredeloup and Pliez, 2006).

Routes

North African routes change constantly and new paths appear every season. Some nodal points in the Sahara remain the same, however. There are three broad routes: the first is from East Africa (Somalia, Ethiopia, Eritrea), through Sudan to Libya. Migrants from the Horn of Africa also cross over the Gulf of Aden to Yemen. It is striking that Yemen in 2006 hosted 88,000 refugees from these countries. The second route is the from West and Central Africa (Liberia, Sierra Leone, Ivory Coast, Burkina Faso, Guinea, Ghana, Cameroon) to Mali and Niger. The route then splits to Libya, or to Algeria and Morocco, or to Mauritania and Morocco. The third route links Morocco through Algeria to Libya and Tunisia, a horizontal corridor for migrants already 'in transit' in the region, who move eastwards or westwards according to rumours about where it is currently easier to cross or where jobs are available. This route is also joined by the Maghrebi.

While usually not included in the analysis of migration in the Maghreb, countries on the West Coast of Africa have recently come to be part of the debate on transit migration to Europe as well, due to the 'diversion' effect of flows traditionally going through Morocco. Stretching right across the Canary islands, Mauritania seems particularly entangled in the transit migration phenomenon. Senegal and Gambia are also new departure points for the Canaries. The numbers of boats leaving has been rising constantly since 2006.

Mauritania's new transit role is due to the increased difficulty of using the route via Morocco (Ba and Choplin, 2005), as well as its ease of access; its frontiers in the south can easily be permeated. Improvement of the road network, which was previously non-existent in the desert, also provides easier access; the road from Dakar through Nouakchott and Nouadhibou to Dakhla in Morocco, or the route from

Nioro in Mali through Ayoun in Mauritania to Dakhla are such examples. The northern Mauritanian border is particularly difficult to control. Nouadhibou is a key port for migrants arriving by boat from West Africa and leaving for the Canary islands. Migrants are also hiding in cargo ships leaving for Europe.

As much as it is difficult and dangerous to cross the Sahara on foot, it remains less mediatized compared to the images of boats crossing the sea to Europe. The Sahara crossing remains one of the most tragic aspects of the human cost of migration to Europe (Collyer, 2006). Between 1996 and 2007 an estimated 1079 people died trying to cross the desert, more than half of them during the last three years.[1] Migrants may spend days or even months in the desert, and they often lose the sense of time or direction. Even smugglers lose their way. Migrants are usually transported by trucks or cars that often break down, leaving migrants to continue the trip on foot.

Certain desert towns are known hubs, where migrants take a break, work to earn some money and find a smuggler or a truck to take them to the north: Gao in Mali, Agadez in Nigeria, Sebha in Libya, Tamanrasset in Algeria (Brechat, 2005). Smugglers are often seen as both agents of exploitation and salvation. As observed in the route through Turkey to Greece the majority of the migrants cannot pay the 'full package' price to get from home to Europe (UNODC, 2006). Smuggling is here, too, organized as a small-scale operation with a few drivers ('guides') involved (UNODC, 2006). The smugglers might collaborate with, or know of, someone involved in delivering fake documents back home – in cities like Conakry, Lagos or Abidjan. They might cover larger distances and link up with other networks of smugglers; they would not, however, constitute a large-scale mafia group (Alioua, 2006; Collyer, 2006; Pastore, Monzini and Sciortino, 2006). It is also common for migrants to get involved in the smuggling business at some point.

The majority of the migrants spend a significant amount of time, sometimes months or years, in the Sahel region before they reach North Africa. It is not a straight journey from A to B. The cost of transportation and fake documents/bribing may be close to a couple of thousand euros, equivalent to a year's salary for some. According to media information, crossing the Sahara may be 1000–3000 euros, depending on the route. A simple crossing through Mali may be 1000 euros.[2] Migrants pay for one leg of the journey at a time and work for months in between.

In fact, transit migration has transformed desert cities, creating activities and income – even if mostly illegal. African markets and shops open up, African meeting points appear in the streets. Pliez (2003) argues that 40 per cent of Sebha in Libya is occupied by sub-Saharans. The south of Algeria has also seen some development lately because of the migrants. And in Nouadhibou they are part of the port economy.

A pattern can be observed, whereby migrants cross the Sahara in autumn/early winter, arrive in North Africa, work in day jobs to earn some money for the next leg of the trip, and usually attempt to cross to Europe in the summer months. It is common to spend a few months or years in the Maghreb before trying to cross the sea. The routes for Europe are the following: the sea route from Tunisia and Libya to Italy (mostly Lampedusa, Pantelleria, Sicily and Sardinia) and to Malta; the sea route from Morocco to the Canary islands or the Spanish coast; the sea route from Mauritania and Senegal to the Canary islands; and finally, the land route from Morocco to the Spanish enclaves of Ceuta and Melilla. The price for the sea trip will be another 1000–2000 euros.

Certain nationalities usually aim for certain destination countries. Algerians usually mention France, the United States, the United Kingdom and Canada as their preferred destination. Some sub-Saharan Africans, like Togolese and Cameroonians may prefer Germany and the Netherlands. Tunisians mention Italy and France. Moroccans prefer Spain, France and Belgium. But the majority follow random travel directions and try their luck up until the next shore. For those that can afford it, the easiest way is to fly to a European destination with a fake passport. This travel option, however, remains rare. Finally, it was recently observed that Asian migrants might also try to reach Europe via Africa as well. In its technical mission to Morocco in 2005, the EC found 130 irregular migrants from India and Bangladesh that seemed to have flown from New Delhi to Bamako in Mali, and then crossed to Mauritania and Morocco. They had paid a total of 6000–8000 euros for the trip. At one point, the Bangladeshis were the biggest group in the reception centre in Ceuta. Similarly, a group of Sri Lankans arrived in the Canary Islands in 2006 with the view of going to Greece. According to the BBC, the cost of migrating from South Asia to Europe via Africa may total 9000–16,000 euros.[3]

The next sections provide an overview of transit migration in Tunisia, Libya, Algeria and Morocco. Particular emphasis is placed on the situation of undocumented migrants and refugees in Morocco during the last couple of years.

Tunisia

A traditional country of emigration, Tunisia still sees many of its youth leaving to seek a better future in Italy and France. The distance from the Tunisian coast to Sicily is merely a stone's throw, often making it irresistible for young Tunisians to try their luck at crossing.

It is not certain how many migrants and refugees are living – temporarily or not – in Tunisia. No official data exist on this topic. In the period 1998–2003 some 20,000 Tunisians and 12,000 foreigners were caught trying to cross the sea from Tunisia to Italy (Bruno Philip, 2003).[4] According to Boubakri (2004), six out of seven of these are Maghrebi. According to another source, between the end of 1998 and the beginning of 2003 the Tunisian authorities apprehended over 37,000 persons crossing the border illegally; 20,000 of these were Tunisians.[5] Flows were larger in the first years after 2000, and the flow continues, even though it seems to have decreased after 2004.

As with most sub-Saharan African migrants in North Africa, migrants in Tunisia are mostly young, male and originating from Central and West Africa. Migrants usually follow the route from Niger through Libya or Algeria to Tunisia. There are also some Moroccans and Algerians who join in the routes, hoping that entry to Europe will be easier this way. The departure points for Sicily and Sardinia are in Nabeul, Sousse, Mahdia and Kelibia. Migrants leaving from Cap Bon usually go for Pantelleria (Mellah, 2000). The smugglers have safe-houses, known as 'gouna', where migrants stay until departure (see Boubakri, 2004). Stories of smugglers dropping migrants off at the Kerkennah Islands instead of Lampedusa have also been reported. The trip to Italy costs between 800 and 1000 euros.[6] One out of five gets caught, the rest manage to reach the other side.

Sub-Saharan African presence is not visible in Tunisia at first sight, with the exception of the 'BADois', the skilled Africans working for the African Development Bank in Tunis. About 1000 staff, together with their family members, constitute a new black community in the city. The contrast is striking between the 'BADois circulating at ease in the city and the undocumented migrants and asylum seekers hiding in certain city pockets. The latter are also said to provide services to the BADois (Boubakri and Mazella, 2005).

There is also a student migration path in Tunisia. 'Fake' and genuine students alike work in the informal economy and often overstay their student visas until the opportunity arises to attempt the crossing to Europe. The majority are single males even though the presence of women is gradually increasing. Others come as sportsmen to work with football clubs in Tunisia; if the contract falls through or expires, they also join the ranks of the undocumented who try to cross to Europe.

Tunisia is party to the 1951 Convention, the 1967 Protocol and the 1969 Organization of African Unity (OAU) Convention. The principle of non-refoulement is enshrined in the Constitution which prohibits extraditing 'political refugees' (Article 17). There is no legislation, however, on refugees, and refugees are subject to the law on foreigners. Decree 75-40 of 1975 on passports and travel documents provides for the delivery of special documents to refugees and stateless persons and on the exemption of refugees from penalties for illegal entry into the territory.

Law 2004-06 of 3 February 2004, amending Law 75-40 of 1975 on passports and travel documents, introduced strict rules to curb the flow of migrants. Tunisia has been active in developing a strong border control force: a police force of 13,000 is also backed by another 12,000 of the National Guard. Joint Italo-Tunisian sea patrols are usually operating in the Messina Strait.[7] Tunisia has also signed and ratified (2003) the UN Smuggling and Trafficking Protocols.

There are no procedures in place to deal with asylum seekers. Instead, it is UNHCR that conducts the refugee status determination, but the residence permits need to be delivered by the state. The number of refugees and asylum seekers registered with UNHCR Tunisia is very small (only 93 refugees and 68 asylum seekers in 2007, van der Klaauw, 2007). In 2000–5 the main refugee nationalities were Algerians, Iraqis and Nigerians. The UNHCR presence is not widely known and newcomers might not be aware of being able to apply in Tunisia. There is a dominant perception in Tunisia, similar to Greece, that refugees are in transit, and therefore do not need asylum in the country. In reality, some are not interested in going to Europe but hope to settle and find protection in Tunisia.

It is not known whether there are reception centres in Tunisia, as no international organization or media are known to have visited any and no data is publicly available on the topic. One could assume that migrants arrested for illegal entry/exit are taken to detention centres along with persons arrested for other offences. News articles make reference to the Ouardia detention centre outside Tunis (Migreurop, 2006) and the Mornaghia prison, where migrants have been reportedly detained for illegal entry.[8] The ICRC, which has been granted authorization to visit persons in detention, might be a potential source of information in the future.[9]

Migrants and refugees are dispersed in houses in the city. Squatting is common and they often change location. Living conditions are below standard and needs seem to be particularly acute in the area of health care. Refugees are catered for by NGOs and Christian church organizations.

Tunisia has also signed a readmission agreement with Italy in 1998, and Austria, Bulgaria, France, Greece, the United Kingdom, Malta and Ukraine.[10] Following Tunisia's ratification of the UN protocol on smuggling, a law penalizing irregular entry/exit and human smuggling was introduced in 2004 (decree 2004/6 amending law 1975). The government's stated aim is to prevent human tragedies at sea, even though some argue that the law essentially aims to penalize not the migrants but young Tunisians who leave in a clandestine manner. It has also been reported that the Tunisian authorities often push migrants to the other side of the Libyan border, including those whose permit has expired; some are handed over to the authorities, others are left in the desert. NGOs often report cases of migrants or refugees who just 'disappeared'.

Tunisia seems more preoccupied with the irregular emigration of its own nationals, which lately seems on the rise; 2500 Tunisians were arrested for illegal entry in European countries in 2005, almost double those in 2004.[11] Despite a bilateral Italy–Tunisia agreement which each year absorbs 3000 Tunisians, more and more there are those that take the irregular path. A great number of families have also declared members missing, most probably drowned in the sea.

A decade ago the profile of Tunisian emigrants was of the poor and most desperate. Today, however, the picture is a bit different; irregular migrants may have completed secondary education or even hold a university degree. They are often stimulated by the 'success' stories of the Tunisian diaspora in France and Italy.

Libya

Libya has been a country of immigration since the 1980s, recruiting African migrants to work in the service, construction and industry sectors. To a large extent this still continues to be the case, as the country continues to present labour opportunities, even if informal most of the time.

The majority of those living and working in Libya come from neighbouring countries. In early 2007, it was estimated that there were over one million sub-Saharan Africans living and working in Libya, over half of which were undocumented.[12] In addition, there is a large community of Egyptians, 323,000 registered in 2005 (Hamood, 2006). More recent estimates put the number of Egyptians close to one million, and Sudanese close to 500,000. There are also 200,000 Moroccans, 20,000–30,000 Algerians and 60,000 Tunisians working in Libya. Many come to Libya with the hope of crossing to Italy. There is also a seasonal trend of 'circular' migration, whereby migrants from neighbouring countries such as Mali, Chad and Niger come to work in the summer months and return to their countries in the winter. The migrant population is predominantly male, even though the number of women has increased considerably over recent years, including that of Nigerian and other nationalities trafficked for prostitution.

Libya has been turning a blind eye on irregular migrants from Africa during the last decade. It is only recently, and in the context of the re-establishment of relations with Europe, that migration has surfaced on the Libyan agenda. In 2006 the number of those undocumented arrested and deported was 64,430.[13] In the same year, Italy arrested 22,000 people who had crossed the sea from Libya, out of which most were Moroccans (8146), Egyptians (4200) and Eritreans (2859).[14] The authorities deported 5046 irregular migrants and arrested over 4000 in only the first half of 2007.[15]

Migrants coming to Libya usually cross the south and east, from Chad, Niger, Sudan or Egypt. There is a route going from the Horn of Africa through Sudan to Libya. Despite the closure of the Sudan–Libya border in 2003, smuggling across the borders seems to have continued unabated. According to Hamood (2006), the cost may be 150,000–450,000 Sudanese pounds (approximately $60–$180). Migrants may spend some time in Sudan before crossing. About 10,000–12,000 people were reported to pass every month from Kufra (border city in southeast Libya) in 2005.

A second route is the horizontal corridor from Morocco through Algeria to Tunisia and Libya. While further from Lampedusa and the Italian coast than Tunisia, Libya is nevertheless a more popular departure area and smuggling is more organized. Regular departure points for Italy are in Zuwarah, Zlitan, Janzur, Sabratha and Benghazi. Migrants use small plastic or fishing boats to cross. The cost of the trip is close to 1500 euros and practices are similar to those described in Chapter 4 for the crossing from the Turkish coast to the Greek islands. As was also observed in Morocco, it seems that many migrants are well aware of the risks of the sea crossing before they attempt it.

Migrants may stay in Libya for years waiting to cross. It is relatively easy to find occasional jobs in Libya and make a living as a transit. The African market in Tripoli is a popular concentration point. Migrants work in construction, services and farming. But life for migrants in Libya is not easy and they have often been victims of racist attacks. Matters relating to migration are regulated by a general framework for laws on third-country nationals. Law 6 of 1987 and its amendments of Law 2 of 1372 (2004) is about the entry, residence and exit of foreigners in Libya. It also covers issues relating to irregular migration and smuggling. In August 2005 there were reports that an additional entry requirement had been introduced obliging people to carry 500 dinars (approximately $400) to cover their expenses during their stay in Libya. Sudanese and Egyptian nationals (and Maghrebi) are not required to obtain a visa.

In an effort to combat irregular migration, the foreign ministry announced in March 2007 that all migrants without a work contract would be deported. Security was also stepped up in the area close to the Tunisian border. Consequently, 36,000 Egyptian workers reportedly returned home at the end of February 2007. Many others crossed to neighbouring countries. While lacking an Association Agreement with the EU, Libya has been collaborating on migration management through EC-funded projects, for example those carried out by IOM with AENEAS funding. Libya has proven quite committed in capacity building of its national authorities and services on migration issues.

At the same time, Libya is the only North African country that has not yet signed the 1951 Convention and its 1967 Protocol; it has, however, signed and ratified the OAU Convention of 1969. This is still an important point considering that some African refugees would not qualify for refugee status strictly under the 1951 Geneva Convention definition, but they could be covered by the 1969 OAU Convention. The Libyan Constitution Proclamation may prohibit the extradition of 'political refugees' (Article 11), yet Libyan laws do not recognize the existence of refugees in the country, and there is no national legislation or administrative procedures in place for asylum.

Few people have lodged an application with UNHCR Libya in the past, but this seems to have changed over the last few years; in early 2007, Libya had 880 refugees and 2000 asylum seekers (van der Klaauw, 2007). There is also a caseload of already settled Palestinians and Somalis. UNHCR is not officially recognized by the government and its presence is also not widely known. In view of the fact that living and working as undocumented is tolerated, refugees may simply wait to cross the sea and seek asylum in Europe. This means, however, that refugees have no access to protection and risk to be detained or deported while in Libya.

There are a number of reception/detention centres in Libya.[16] Italy is known to have financed one detention centre outside Tripoli, and pledges were made for two more.[17] Human rights groups have frequently denounced detention conditions for being in breach of human rights. Police round-ups and forced and voluntary returns are common. It is reported that over 20,000 people were deported during the three-year period 2002–4; Human Rights Watch puts the figure much higher at 145,000 in 2003–5 (Human Rights Watch, 2006). Italy funded the repatriation of 5688 people from Libya to their countries of origin in 2003–4.

Italy's position is instrumental in this case. Italy is a major destination and transit country and a major actor in migration management in the Mediterranean. According to MPI data, in 2003 the country was host to 1.5 million registered migrants, with top nationalities being Albanian (171,567) Moroccan (170,746) and Romanian (close to 950,000).[18] Another 2.4 million is estimated to be living and working illegally (Giacca, 2004). For a number of years, Italy's single response to irregular migration was regularization; seven regularization programmes were carried out in the last 20 years. The latest one in 2003 regularized 634,728 migrants and was the biggest programme ever conducted in Europe. The majority of the regularized were more or less from the same nationalities as those registered. Combating irregular migration has been supplemented with readmission agreements with various origin and transit countries. The Italian approach to cooperation for migration management has also been combined with bilateral agreements with third countries, offering quotas and other forms of admission, particularly for seasonal work. Such agreements exist, for example, with Albania, Moldova, Tunisia, Morocco, Egypt, Nigeria, Sri Lanka, Bangladesh and Pakistan.

As far as Libya is concerned, following the lifting of the arms embargo in 2004 cooperation has focused considerably on technical and financial support for border control, surveillance and capacity building for migration management. The two countries also signed an agreement for cooperation in the fight against irregular migration (2004). Italy has also resorted to deportations and returns as a response to migrant arrivals. Pastore and Sciortino (2003) estimate that between 1998 and 2002 an average of 40,000 migrants were expelled annually. Several hundred migrants were deported from Italy to Libya between October 2004 and March 2005, including cases of refugees that were not granted access to asylum. Human rights groups and the international community criticized heavily the policy of mass deportations, particularly regarding the lack of protection safeguards in Libya and the risk of refugees being returned to their countries of origin. The same type of collective expulsions continued well into

2005. In September 2005 a European Parliament delegation visited the island of Lampedusa to assess the situation on the ground and found that migrants did not have access to asylum procedures in Lampedusa and were being forcibly returned to Libya (European Parliament, 2005).

Algeria

Transit migration flows through Algeria date back to the late 1980s and early 1990s. Yet, Algeria – and Europe – never seemed very preoccupied with it, and it is only now that the topic seems to be coming out in the news. In the period 2000–3, the gendarmerie arrested 11,197 irregular migrants. There were even nine Bangladeshis among them.[19] This detail is an indication that complex transit routes had already developed through Algeria even before the other Maghreb neighbours came under the spotlight.

On the other hand, Algeria has only recently become a transit/destination space in the sense that sub-Saharan migrants may stay and work in the country (Hammouda, 2005). This is mostly a result of the restoration of peace and relative security and economic growth. Algeria now presents all kinds of job opportunities; controlling its enormous borders in the South is also more difficult than in Morocco or Tunisia. Algeria is also a destination country for Tunisians who might also work as undocumented.[20]

Migrants usually gather in cities like Tamanrasset, Adrar, Illizi, Tlemcen, Oran and Algiers. Usual departure points are Constantine, Oran, Tarifa and beaches along the coast up to the Moroccan border. Leaving Algeria, migrants either go westwards to Spain or eastwards to Italy; 16,000 migrants crossed from Algeria to the Gibraltar straights in 2006. The price to cross may be between 70,000–100,000 Algerian Dinars (750–1000 euros).

It has been reported that migrants in Algeria also get involved in other types of smuggling and trafficking activities, like drugs. The country also seems to have become a hub for men, women, and children from sub-Saharan Africa and Asia trafficked for forced labour and prostitution. Some are coerced or trapped in a trafficking relation, others might consciously be involved to make ends meet. Migrants transiting in the country who were not trafficked might also become victims of forced prostitution and domestic servitude in an attempt to earn money for the next leg of the trip (US Department of State, 2006). It is no coincidence that a sharp increase in HIV infection is currently observed in Tamanrasset (Home Office, 2006). According to an article in the Algerian magazine *L'Expression*, during the past decade the state was too preoccupied with combating political violence internally to really pay any attention to irregular migration, drug smuggling and human trafficking networks that were gradually taking roots in the country.[21]

African communities are visible and established in the Algerian South. Tamanrasset, in particular seems to be experiencing a new era of population growth with all kinds of African groups circulating in the city, a situation last seen at the time of the caravans.

At the same time, Algeria has been a refugee hosting country for a number of decades, accommodating over 100,000 Sahrawi (Western Saharan) refugees in the southwest, around the Tindouf region. The Sahrawi refugees arrived in Algeria in 1976 after Spain withdrew from the Western Sahara and a conflict started with Morocco over control of the territory. Most of them have been living in these camps ever since. This refugee topic seems to have dominated the agenda (and foreign policy) in Algeria. In contrast, the small caseload of urban refugees from other countries (175 refugees and 950 asylum seekers in early 2007) is not attracting much attention. Yet, in late 2006 UNHCR in Algeria started to receive on average 100 asylum applications per month (van der Klaauw, 2007). There is also a population of 4500 Palestinians long settled and integrated in the country. Algeria has signed the 1951 UN Convention, the 1967 Protocol and the 1969 OAU Convention. The Ministry of Interior is the state body responsible for refugee issues.

Algeria has signed readmission agreements with Germany, Bulgaria, Belgium, Spain, France, Italy, Luxembourg, Malta, the Netherlands and the United Kingdom. Similar to Morocco, Algeria also claims to be burdened with sub-Saharan African migration, without, however, receiving substantial EU assistance – or at least not as much as the other Maghreb countries. From its side, Morocco often accuses Algeria of harbouring human smuggling and pushing irregular migrants over the border to Morocco. It is likely that many of these debates also stem from the two countries' deep political rivalry and strained bilateral relations. It is, however, possible that they also contain elements of truth. Morocco does seem to monopolize much of the media attention. And it has often been reported in the news that Algeria deports or abandons migrants at the Sahara border: 6092 were sent to In Guezzam (border with Niger) and Tin Zaouatine (border with Mali) in the period 2000–3; 20,000 migrants were deported between 2001 and 2006.[22]

Morocco

Morocco is a major emigration country. Today the number of Moroccans living abroad is estimated at close to three million, out of which two million in Western Europe (de Haas, 2005). Remittances are one of the main sources of income in the country. Migrating to Europe remains popular and emigration continues unabated.

At the same time, Morocco is a country of transit and destination. This transformation is not as new as it seems. During the 1990s it is estimated that over 1600 smuggling networks were identified and disrupted and more than 65,000 people arrested (Charef, 2004). Morocco was already in European focus in 1999, as is proved by the existence of a HLWG Morocco Action Plan. Yet, in recent years the scale of the phenomenon and a number of tragic incidents have brought Morocco centre stage; 26,000 irregular migrants are estimated to have arrived in Morocco between 2002–4.[23] A total of 21,894 irregular migrants were apprehended in Morocco only in 2005 (UNODC, 2006).

Migrating for study purposes is an important migration vector. About 10,000 sub-Saharan Africans were enrolled as students in Morocco in 2005; they all enter and remain in the country legally. Nevertheless, during or after the termination of their studies it is common to remain in Morocco or attempt to cross illegally to Europe. Another legal migration channel to Morocco is through sports clubs. These two practices may bring in small numbers of people at a time, yet they create a nucleus of communities that serve as resources supporting other sub-Saharans (including the undocumented).

African communities are visible in the big cities of Casablanca and Rabat.[24] It seems that more and more sub-Saharan Africans eventually settle in Morocco. They seem more preoccupied with how to improve their living conditions in that country, rather than crossing to Spain. Contrary to the situation in Greece, this is neither a result of informal integration through employment, nor is it a result of obtaining asylum or other type of residence permit. It is also not a process of informal, social integration in the transit country. Instead, it is a matter of getting 'stuck' for a number of reasons, from the lack of policies to the lack of resources, and being unable to move on or return home. The more they stay, the more diverse policy issues come to the surface, like access to employment, health care and schooling for the migrant children, which still remain unresolved.

The overwhelming majority arrive in Morocco from Algeria, crossing from Maghnia over to Oujda.[25] The southern border with Mauritania is more difficult to cross, due to mines, heavy patrolling, and the particular security situation prevailing as a result of the unresolved Western Sahara issue. Up to 2005, it was common to cross from Laayoune to the Canary Islands or mainland Spain. Moroccans trying to emigrate join in the same route through the Canary Islands, or try the alternative route through Libya. In 2005 alone, 368 people lost their lives trying to cross to Spain.[26] According to Collyer (2004), many are aware of the risks involved in crossing the sea before they attempt it. Still, they are not deterred by the fact that others perished. It's either cross, or die. As will be explained in the next section, a number of incidents triggered a control 'craze' in Morocco in 2005–6, which resulted in intensified land and sea patrols and a drop in numbers crossing to Spain in early 2006. Yet in summer 2006, the flow increased again. This time the migrants reached the Canaries with 'cayucos' of 80–90 people from Mauritania, Senegal and Gambia. They spent over 15 days on the water in these vessels. According to the European Parliament LIBE Committee's visit to the Canaries in July 2006, the migrants are usually transferred to the Spanish mainland a few days later (European Parliament, 2006d).

In Morocco migration issues are regulated by law 02-03 of 2003. The law regulates the entry and exit of foreigners and codifies crimes and penalties relating to irregular migration and human smuggling, making them criminal offences. The law also makes reference to the international conventions Morocco has signed, including the International Convention on the Protection of the Rights of All Migrant Workers and Members of Their Families, ratified in 2003. Morocco has not yet ratified the UN Smuggling and Trafficking Protocols (2000). Morocco has signed readmission agreements with Germany, Spain, France, Italy, Malta and Portugal, and it has also signed agreements with countries of origin, such as Mali and Senegal. Seven thousand guards are known to be currently deployed in the northern frontier zone, plus additional numbers in Nador and in Tetouan. Two bodies within the Ministry of Interior were set up in 2003, the Migration and Border Surveillance Directorate and the Migration Monitoring Centre to support the fight against irregular migration and trafficking.[27]

In the area of asylum, Morocco has signed and ratified the 1951 Convention, the 1967 Protocol and the 1969 OAU Convention. The 2003 migration law partly provides for residence permits for refugees (Article17), even though they would need to have somehow already secured legal residence.[28] The 'Bureau des Refugiés et Apatrides', Ministry of Foreign Affairs, established since 1957, grants residence status to refugees under UNHCR mandate. There is currently no asylum law, and no procedure for registering an asylum claim directly with the Moroccan government. UNHCR conducts the refugee status determination process and issues 'attestations' to registered asylum seekers. The government does not really acknowledge the presence of refugees in the country; the official position being that due to their irregular means of entry, asylum seekers and refugees registered with UNHCR are irregular migrants. Should they need protection, the argument seems to go, they could have sought this in the countries they transited on their way to Morocco (van der Klaauw, 2007).

At the beginning of 2007, 500 refugees and 1300 asylum seekers were registered with UNHCR Rabat. The year before, the office had processed more than 1700 asylum applications (van der Klaauw, 2007). Most asylum seekers are from the Democratic Republic of Congo (DRC), Congo-Brazzaville, the Ivory Coast, Nigeria and Liberia.

No provisions exist for the reception of asylum seekers in the country. For a long time, transit migrants (including refugees) would hide in villages and in the forest area of Gourougou and Ben Younesh until these settlements were dismantled in 2005. The reopening of the UNHCR office in Rabat (previously in Casablanca) in 2005 seems to have triggered a movement from the countryside to the capital; many seek to apply for asylum, even if no genuine claim is present. Many are also concentrated around Oujda close to the Algerian border. Registered asylum seekers lack residence and work permits, like the irregular migrants. They live with the constant fear of being arrested and deported. UNHCR often faces incidents where registered asylum seekers are arrested and their documents confiscated. Their financial situation and living conditions are particularly bad, and begging is common. Finding a job, even occasional day jobs, is not evident in a poor country like Morocco. It should be noted, however, that progress has been made recently, as the state now grants refugees access to health care, schooling and vocational training (André and Charlet, 2007). UNHCR and the Moroccan government signed an accord de siege in July 2007. UNHCR also tries to support durable solutions for refugees through self-reliance, resettlement with certain member states and voluntary return.

While refugees are not a popular topic, combating irregular migration certainly is in Morocco. Moroccans seem particularly concerned about becoming a destination country because of their geographical location. As we saw in Chapter 2, cooperation with Europe in migration management is anticipated in the association agreement. Yet,

Morocco has not been particularly fast in taking steps in this area – at least not before the events of 2005 in Ceuta and Melilla attracted international attention. At the same time, Morocco commonly claims to be overburdened with sub-Saharan African migration, more than any other country in North Africa, using this argument to lobby for further assistance.

By far the biggest external impact on transit migration has to do with policy developments in Spain (and vice versa). In 2001 the foreign-born population in Spain was 1,109,060, with the Moroccans (234,937) being the biggest community (Ortega-Perez, 2003). But it is the use of Morocco as a transit route that has the biggest effect on this relation (although it is worth underlining that the majority of Spain's illegal migrants have entered legally and then overstayed). The history of Spanish migration policy shares much with the Greek one. Immigration to Spain increased rapidly in the last decade, and irregular migration is equally large; the number of undocumented migrants was estimated at 1.2 million in 2004 (Arango and Jachimowicz, 2005). Like Greece, too, it has taken Spain some time to develop adequate policy responses. Spain has also frequently been resorting to regularization and has carried out six programmes since 1986, the last and more sophisticated having taken place in 2005 (Papadopoulou, 2005b). Spain has also invested in border control and since 1999 has a highly developed technical system, the SIVE, in place for the surveillance of external borders. Yet the system has not managed to reduce migration flows; instead, smugglers invented new routes, took faster boats and, as Carling (2007b) explains, even accepted the possibility of being caught. It is worth noting that SIVE has at the same time also provided assistance to boats in distress, saving human lives.

As with Italy, much of the debate in Spain has centred around deportations and forced repatriations. According to Alscher (2005) Spain has been repatriating an average of 25,000 migrants annually since 1994. The Spanish human rights association APDH reports that 10,635 migrants were repatriated in 2006 (up to 30 October), almost half of them to Morocco (APDH, 2007). Spain has been criticized for this policy and particularly for the lack of respect for the principle of non-refoulement.

Having outlined the main transit routes through the African continent and the overall migration situation in the four Maghreb countries, the next section goes into more depth in order to analyse the case of transit migrants in Morocco.

5.2   Transit in Morocco

A few years ago, irregular migrants in Morocco used to hide in the forest, in makeshift settlements made out of cardboard and plastic. The most well known were those of Gourougou and Ben Younesh in the north, close to the Spanish enclaves of Ceuta and Melilla. Seven migrant 'settlements' were known to be existing in the country in 2003–4, including the university campus in Oujda and shanty towns around Casablanca, Rabat and Laayoune. Through hearsay, Gourougou and Ben Younesh became quite popular and hosted from 500–800 up to 2000-3000 sub-Saharan migrants at times.

The homeless migrants lived in horrible conditions; they would not have survived if it was not for local human rights associations and activists, and regular visits paid by Médecins sans Frontières. The French NGO Cimade conducted field research in the informal 'camps' back in 2004 and its report remains a precious source of information on the transit conditions in Morocco at that time. According to Cimade, almost all African nationalities were represented in the camps, with Nigerians being the majority. The migrants were divided in 'sub-groups' and 'committees' on the basis of ethnic groups or language (French or English speakers). The population was predominantly male. Some of them had been living there for five to six years. It took most of them significant amounts of time to reach Morocco, and by that time they had run out of energy and resources to continue any further. They were waiting in the camps for the opportunity to cross the fence separating the Spanish enclaves Ceuta and Melilla from the Moroccan mainland. Those who could afford it travelled to Laayoune in the south to take 'pateras' (boats) and cross to the Canary Islands. Most of them spent over a year in the settlement.

Raids in the camps were common and migrants were usually taken to Oujda, close to the Algerian border. They would all return to the camps on foot a few days later. According to Cimade, those with economic motivations were the most keen to cross to Europe; on the contrary, persons in need of protection had no particular destinations in mind and all they wanted was to apply for asylum, wherever that would be possible. Nevertheless, living conditions in Morocco did not leave migrants and refugees much to hope for, and eventually almost everyone preferred to cross to Europe. Cimade's assessment was that about half of the population was potentially eligible for refugee status. The UNHCR office (in Casablanca at the time) was neither known nor active, and seeking asylum in Morocco was not considered a realistic option.

It is evident that Morocco was not particularly interested in managing transit migration at that time. As long as they were hiding in the bushes the sub-Saharans were invisible. A weak UNHCR presence and few asylum applications meant that asylum was a non-issue. Moreover, as long as Morocco was not facing European (and particularly Spanish) pressures, the issue was not on the agenda.

The camps of Gourougou and Ben Younesh were dismantled in 2005 following Moroccan raiding operations. Following the raids, some sub-Saharans moved to the cities. It was also around that time that the UNHCR office closed in Casablanca and reopened in Rabat, this time more dynamic and present than before. Most sub-Saharans rushed to lodge an application, including many with no genuine need for protection, who hoped that the registration note would secure some stability and protection. The number of asylum seekers boomed from 177 pending cases in 2003 to 1897 new applicants in 2005, creating a backlog of 2000 cases.[29]

The migrants gradually gathered in the shanty towns of Rabat and Casablanca. Constant raids and arrests, unemployment and the prospect of not having a shelter for the coming winter put substantial pressure on the migrants, who saw crossing over the fences as the only solution. The idea of organizing a collective attempt started circulating in the groups. While some had tried and failed this before, it was thought that a massive attempt would provide enough forces to counter the Spanish Guardia Civil. A first attempt was made in August 2005 in Melilla and cost one migrant his life. It had a snowball effect. In the night of 28/29 September, 500 migrants equipped with gloves and ladders moved to Ceuta and, divided in five groups, they tried to cross the double security barrier. Five migrants died. The news hit the headlines around the world, bringing Morocco and transit migration to the centre of attention. The live footage of migrants jumping over the barrier of an international border had a direct effect on policy instincts. A second mass attempt was followed only ten days later, in early October with 700 migrants trying to scale the security barriers, this time in Melilla. Six of them died. In total, 135 Africans, four police officers and three soldiers were injured in the event;[30] 350 entered Melilla, the remaining half, however, were forced back by Spanish police and were taken by the Moroccans to the Algerian border.

Those that managed to cross were readmitted back to Morocco using a pre-existing readmission agreement, the 'Accord de Malaga' of 1992, unused up to that date. According to UNHCR, among those readmitted were also asylum seekers and some who might have been eligible for asylum. They were also taken to the Algerian border close to Nador, where the others were concentrated. It is estimated that in total over 1500 were taken to the border. Another group was taken 2000 km down to the south, even though Moroccan authorities claimed to have sent them to Oujda. It was journalists and NGOs that spotted 25 buses packed with migrants heading south. It is reported that they were stripped of their money and mobile phones and left in the desert without food and provisions.

The public outcry about the deaths and the scandal about migrants abandoned in the desert mobilized international NGOs and media, and the EU sent a team of experts to assess the situation. About 1500 migrants were spotted by NGOs near the village of Ain Chouettar in southern Morocco. They had been transported to military barracks close to Guelmime (Bouizakarn, Dakhla). After almost a month left in the desert, 73 migrants started a hunger strike. UNHCR tried to gain access to the camp as it became known that there were registered asylum seekers among them. A refugee status determination procedure was conducted on the spot, and those identified as genuine claimants were released. UNHCR was not, however, allowed to access the western camp in Taouima, Nador, where the other group was concentrated.

Morocco organized repatriations to Mali, Nigeria and Senegal on the basis of existing repatriation agreements with these countries. Over 20 flights were organized in the following month for hundreds of migrants in addition to returns aboard commercial flights. Apparently this was not the first time Morocco had applied the measure of repatriation flights. Collyer (2004) mentions that a year before these events, in 2004, Morocco had conducted six such flights to Nigeria.

Nationals of other countries were reportedly taken into detention, or abandoned in the desert. A few days later, the remaining migrants in Nador were ushered onto buses and taken to Algeria. Some managed to cross back to Morocco, others gathered in Maghnia (on the Algerian side of the border). It was reported that, in turn, the Algerians deported many of them to Mali.

The story of Ceuta and Melilla made waves in the international community, bringing the tragedy of transit migrants to the forefront. Morocco was criticized for the deportations, repatriations and its treatment of migrants abandoned in the desert. It also triggered control 'hype' in Morocco, Spain and the EU as a whole. Morocco deployed 8500 additional border guards around Ceuta and Melilla, and Spain posted another 500 on the other side. The next summer the EU invested heavily in sea patrol operations off the Moroccan coast. Nevertheless, tighter controls hardly affected sub-Saharan migrations that simply changed routes. The number of 'pateras' leaving the Moroccan coast decreased, but as mentioned earlier, it shifted to the coast of Mauritania and Senegal. In total, the number of Africans reaching the Canary Islands in 2006 was double that of 2005. Arrests and detention of asylum seekers continued in Morocco throughout 2005 and 2006.

Furthermore, the events of 2005 had a visible impact on the overall policy approach to migration in Morocco. Neglect gave place to a strong interest and political will to combat irregular migration. It is no surprise that Morocco took the initiative to organize the summit on EU–Africa migration in Rabat in the summer of 2006. The image Morocco was projecting outside became a particular concern.[31]

A year later, at the end of 2006, another set of raids were carried out in the shanty towns of Rabat where migrants were gathering, and 240 were reportedly arrested. One-third were said to hold UNHCR documents. As previously, they were stripped of documents and taken to the border, then they returned to Oujda. Following UNHCR intervention, document holders were allowed to return to Rabat.[32] In other words, despite the international summit and fresh interest in migration management, Morocco still applied the old method of raids and transportation to the border in a typical 'not in my backyard' approach. Many of the repatriated migrants then migrated back to Morocco for a second time.

While the situation in Morocco might display some similarities to that described in Greece, it does so in a more repressive fashion. The migrants and refugees are significantly worse off, as they get 'stuck' in a precarious situation for some time. According to migrant accounts from various sources, it usually takes 15–20 months on average to reach Morocco from sub-Saharan Africa. News articles often make reference to the migrants' courage and determination to continue the journey at any cost. One should, however, also make reference to the anxiety, frustration, the fear for one's life and the fear of the water, and often, the lack of will to continue, as explained in the previous chapter. Many are 'stuck' in Morocco because of those factors. In addition, some have the 'burden' of a family depending on their migration. This factor might be as strong a deterrent to return as the question of survival or protection back home.

As in Greece, some have a particular destination in mind when leaving their country, but many others do not. Some had not imagined they would go that far. But after a few years in Morocco and with no end in sight, most migrants see no other prospect but crossing to

Europe. Unlike Greece, where undocumented migrants find ways to earn a living and asylum seekers have access to employment, in Morocco it seems very hard to make ends meet. The lack of permits means lack of access to the labour market as well as health care and education. Constant police raids and deportations and the inability to obtain legal status put them in a particularly vulnerable position. Refugees, in particular, find themselves in a helpless position, as protection standards in the country (and in the region overall) are almost non-existent.

Earlier in the book, I described the limit between transit and settlement as the degree to which a migrant engages with the structures and opportunities in the receiving country. In the case of Morocco, it can be said that only a few migrants reach the point of settlement in that sense. Yet thousands of migrants do end up staying in the country for years. Although this might appear counter-intuitive at first, in the context of transit migration, settlement and duration of stay are two different issues. The logic that if a country prevents settlement, then the duration of stay will be shrunk to insignificant levels is one that does not stand the test of reality. Many policy attempts based on this assumption (including in Greece and in Morocco) are here to demonstrate this.

The situation is constantly changing for migrants transiting in Morocco. Five years ago they would hide in the bushes and pray for their survival. Today, whether they are still undocumented or registered with UNHCR (but lacking work and residence permits), there is a web of 'support structures' coming to their assistance and advocating for their rights. Both Moroccan and international advocacy groups, human rights activists and associations, international and local NGOs, churches and compatriots provide resources and build a platform for advocacy. A recent publication in the magazine *Autrepart* (2007) described how even religious networks all along the routes from the Sahel to the Mediterranean coast also provide assistance and socialization opportunities for transit migrants. This has grown considerably after the events of Ceuta and Melilla. As a result migrants in Morocco are also more dynamic and vocal than elsewhere in North Africa and have formed their own associations.[33] It needs to be acknowledged that despite the state's restrictive and reluctant stance, Moroccan civil society is free to advocate its goals and support the migrants. These activist structures are not accompanied, however, by public sympathy for the refugee cause. In fact, the public remains either ignorant or indifferent towards the refugees.

The presence and function of an UNHCR office has also changed the landscape and dynamics of transit migration in Morocco. Asylum was a non-issue up to the re-opening of the UNHCR office in Rabat in 2004–5. Since then, the number of persons presenting themselves to the office has boomed. This increase is definitely a sign that there are indeed refugees living in Morocco who need to receive protection in the country. On the other hand, it is also a sign of asylum abuse and the migrants' need to secure some kind of document and shield themselves against deportation. In the absence of a proper asylum framework and repressive police practices against the undocumented, the UNHCR office has in their eyes become symbolic of an all-in-one authority compensating for the state. The sub-Saharans see UNHCR as both an agent of salvation and control: even the screening of applications and rejection of unfounded cases is seen as a sign of state repression. Civil society activists also take a rather paradoxical stance whereby they both denounce UNHCR as being Europe's 'externalization' actor in Morocco and also request that the office provides financial resources and registration papers to all. Sit-ins, hunger strikes and protests have been regular incidents outside the Rabat office in the last two years.[34]

For its part, Morocco has proved reluctant to develop a framework for asylum and to protect the refugees found in its territory, out of fear that this would act as a pull factor. To some extent these fears are realistic. They should not, however, diminish the need to deliver protection to those found in the country, as this stems from Morocco's international human rights and protection obligations. At the same time, it is certain that Morocco would be more forthcoming in the area of asylum if there were more signs of 'burden sharing' from the European side, specifically through resettlement in Europe. Only 20 refugees from Morocco were resettled in Europe (Spain and Portugal) in the year 2006 (van der Klaauw, 2007).

Migration routes are constantly changing in this part of the world. At the same time, North African countries are gradually becoming destination countries, as the number of migrants and refugees stranded in the region increases. Migrant categories are particularly mixed in North Africa. Migrants float between the undocumented, asylum seekers, students, tourists, workers or mandated refugees, taking it as it comes. While the reasons for leaving their country may be clearly forced, life in transit soon creates economic hardships making the refugees' economic needs more pronounced. It is also the other way round: migrants who might leave their country in search of a better life may suffer from inhuman treatment, violation of human rights or torture, even become victims of trafficking and turn to a state where they need protection. It is often hard to draw a distinction between forced and voluntary migration in these mixed transit flows, which in itself makes the granting of effective protection difficult. It also depends on whether 'protection' is based on a narrow or broad application of the refugee definition, for example one closer to the OAU Convention.[35]

There is also a closer relation and overlap between categories and groups, who often support each other, providing money, assistance for accommodation or fake documents for the next journey. It is in this context that the university campus in Oujda became intrinsically involved in the sub-Saharan migration. Sub-Saharans transiting in North Africa share a consciousness of being in transit, similar to, but also different from, the transit migrants in Greece. Not only are they between places, they also share the bonding of a black community clearly distinguished from the host society (migrants and blacks are often seen in the region as synonymous).

Following the Ceuta and Melilla events, Europe became particularly concerned about the African migration flows coming through Morocco. However, European perspectives do not really see the complexities of transit migration in the region: flows that are substantially mixed and where migrants shift frequently between categories, refugees fleeing violent conflict in Africa, a constant threat of forced return, harsh living conditions, unemployment, poverty and lack of access to health care, racism, lack of state capacities, exploitation in prostitution or forced labour in the Sahara. Refugees and asylum seekers lack the minimum level of legal security and it is hard to see how they can rebuild their lives in North Africa at present. Ceuta and Melilla are only the tip of the iceberg: there is a lot more going on in the region.

6
Transit in the East: Shifting Borders

6.1   Mobility patterns in the East in the 1990s

At the turn of the century and in the years 2000–4 there was a proliferation of studies on migration in Central and Eastern Europe. Scholars tended to argue that these countries were a new or 'emerging' migration space (see, for example, Wallace and Stola, 2001; Gorny and Ruspini, 2004). In fact, as this chapter will show, migration, and transit migration in particular, was not as new as presented. Instead, there was a tradition of transit migration in the region. Evidently, the disintegration of the Soviet Union and the communist regime and the turmoil that followed increased migration flows substantially. Nevertheless, it was not the transit migration that increased, compared to previous years; it was the creation of external borders and the introduction of visas that turned internal movements international, making them subject to controls and, to a large extent, irregular.

This tradition of transit migration can be explained, amongst others, by usual practices of movement in the region in search of better opportunities, often on a seasonal or temporary basis. There was also a tradition of migrating for study purposes. People were moving between the Soviet Republics and between Eastern European countries for a number of reasons and this was never a migration issue, and never had any such policy implications. In addition, suitcase traders and vendors crossing borders were a very standard practice in the region. The street-market tradition is also relevant to this transit migration and trade pattern, going back to Soviet times. Markets have been providing informal and day jobs for migrants for a number of years. Recently it was estimated that up to 20,000 non-Russians were working in the Moscow markets alone (even if many were doing so illegally). All this makes transit migrants an integral part of the social fabric. The whole region was a large transit space for all kinds of activities, many of which, however, were not necessarily related to Europe (or had no further destination prospect in Europe).

Furthermore, the transit movements were not subject to visas. Crossing borders was easy and borders were internal, separating families and friends only on the map. There were loopholes and possibilities allowing movement and temporary residence. At the same time emigration to and immigration from abroad was not allowed and the republics remained isolated from the international community. In addition, transit migrants were not necessarily vulnerable in the same way as is witnessed today. There were no deaths at the frontiers and frontiers were open, which also meant that migrants did not resort to the services of smugglers to cross the border. Transit migrants were also not getting stuck in the region; the sense of being 'stuck' appeared in the mid- to late 1990s, as it became difficult to cross the borders. It is only after irregular migration gained policy relevance in Europe that transit migration also gained policy relevance in Eastern Europe.

There is also a long history of smuggling goods and people and trafficking drugs in the whole region from Central Asia up to the European border. There are established routes and large populations that depend on this for their daily living; so the transit or other types of movements have also followed the track of these routes. In addition, all this is coupled to a large tradition of ethnic minorities moving to countries of their ethnic origin. This was particularly strong as soon as the Soviet Union collapsed, for fear of discrimination or political pressure. Ethnic Ukrainians moved (back) to Ukraine, ethnic Latvians to Latvia, ethnic Russians to Russia and so on.

Eastern Europe and the CIS have also been source and host countries to large numbers of forced migrants. The political events in Eastern Europe in 1989 also led to the displacement of refugees, culminating in the war in former Yugoslavia. Almost 700,000 refugees fled to Western Europe in 1992, the biggest refugee crisis in Europe since World War II. Germany received almost half of them. Being in the immediate vicinity, Hungary, the Czech Republic, Poland and Slovenia also received a large share of the asylum seekers throughout the 1990s and for the next years up to EU accession. In Hungary, for example, it is estimated that almost 40,000 arrived in the 1990s (Juhasz, 1999). The number of Balkan refugees increased further in the late 1990s. Around 350,000 people became internally displaced in Kosovo and another 450,000 ethnic Albanians left for Albania, 250,000 to the Former Yugoslav Republic of

Macedonia and 70,000 to Montenegro in 1998–9. Many of those returned home after 1999, but left again a few years later.

The collapse of the Soviet Union and the political conflicts that erupted in many border areas, such as in the Transnistria, in Nagorno-Karabagh, or North Ossetia, also produced large numbers of IDPs and refugees. 360,000 ethnic Armenians are known to have crossed to Azerbaijan in the 1990s; an estimated 360,000 Chechen refugees are internally displaced in Russia.

There has also been a migration of Southeast Asians to Eastern Europe and the former Soviet Union. In the Czech Republic, the Vietnamese community arrived back in the 1970s and 1980s, through programmes provided by the country as a form of aid to Vietnamese and other communist countries. The same is also the case in Bulgaria, again with the Vietnamese who back in the 1980s were the only foreign labour force in the country. These were soon followed by Arabs (in the 1970s and 1980s) and Chinese in the 1980s. In Hungary, the Chinese came and settled in the late 1980s/early 1990s. All these migrations have created migrant communities that are now in place and provide support structures to newcomers.

The borders have shifted many times during the last 15 years, including also the European borders following the two enlargements in 2004 and 2007. Internal borders became external, and countries that were previously in the middle of a vast state or a homogeneous group of states, now found themselves to be Europe's gatekeepers, or its immediate neighbours. As borders have been changing, so have the flows of people and the routes they take.

The countries can be grouped together into three 'sub-regions' in terms of migration systems: the new member states of Eastern Europe, the CIS countries and the Balkans. But even within these sub-regions it is hard to identify common characteristics. There are large disparities in terms of job markets, employment rates, demographic growth and economic development.

Today the Balkans and the CIS are Europe's new neighbours. The CIS in particular is now the transit region par excellence. Asians and Africans are transiting through the Central Asian republics, Russia and Ukraine, and usually spend large amounts of time on the way. Some estimates put the number in thousands, others in millions of people. These neighbours are at one and the same time both transit and destination countries. Russia is also a major destination, second only to the United States in terms of foreign born population. Kazakhstan hosts large numbers of labour migrants. The new member states of Eastern and Central Europe are also origin, transit and destination countries.

The next section will present the situation of transit migration in Eastern Europe and the CIS during the 1990s and up to EU enlargement in 2004. I will then examine the impact of EU enlargement and finally close with a study of Europe's current Eastern neighbours and the routes followed by transit migrants through the Black Sea and Central Asia today.

Transit migration in the 1990s

The collapse of the Soviet Union and communist regimes opened the borders to the West and changed the landscape by creating new external borders in the region. This, together with the overall improvement of communication and transportation triggered off migration flows in all directions. It is striking that today almost one-third of all third-country nationals living in the EU originate from Eastern European, Balkan countries and the Russian Federation.

First of all, political change and decline in economic and living standards in the years since 1991 triggered substantial emigration from Eastern and Central Europe to the West. Ukraine was one of the major migrant-producing countries. In the early years of the 1990s, Ukraine received almost two million ethnic Ukrainians from other CIS countries. With no employment prospects, most of them left the country within a couple of years, joined also by many locals. Large numbers settled in Poland, Russia, in Southern Europe (Greece, Spain and Portugal), Canada and Argentina. Today Portugal hosts over 200,000 Ukrainians. The size and sudden character of these flows is indeed impressive; from 127 Ukrainians in Portugal in 1997 they had already reached 65,000 in 2002 (Malynovska, 2006).

Moldova is another country that saw its children leaving one after the other, a flow that continues unabated to this day. It is estimated that more than 90 per cent of young people in Moldova are eager to go abroad. Emigration from Moldova exceeds the most pessimistic scenarios. According to Moldovan estimates, 25 per cent of the population is working abroad, most illegally (Jandl, 2003). Popular destinations are Italy, Spain, Portugal and Greece. Turkey is also a popular destination, particularly for the Turkic Gagauz minority. The situation is also similar in Georgia, where between 300,000 and 1.5 million people have emigrated during the last ten years, mainly to the United States, Greece, Germany, France, Belgium and Turkey (van Selm, 2005b). Between 1991 and 2004 over 2.5 million people emigrated from Ukraine, mainly to

Eastern and Western Europe, Turkey and the United States. Large emigration created a demographic gap in these countries. On the other hand, Georgia, Moldova and Ukraine are today among the most remittance-dependent countries in the world. They have also concluded labour recruitment agreements with the West.

Introducing visas between some countries, for example between some Eastern European and Central Asian/Black Sea countries was another consequence of the change of borders. Crossing borders was now more difficult and migrants increasingly turned to smugglers and the use of fake documents. Traditional intra-regional movements for all kinds of purposes were now 'international migrations' and traditional transit activities were transformed into irregular transit migrations. At the same time, an increasing number of persons moved to Eastern Europe but unlike previous transit migrations, this time the aim was to go to Western Europe. That was particularly the case for countries like Hungary, the Czech Republic or Poland which were on the route to Germany and Austria, both very popular destinations at the time. It was around that time also that European and international organizations became interested in the issue of transit migration in Eastern Europe, evident in the series of IOM studies carried out in the mid-1990s.

On the other hand, countries like Kazakhstan and the rest of Central Asian republics were not on the map of irregular migrations at that time and only picked up after EU enlargement. Kazakhstan was primarily an emigration country, hosting only a few migrants from Mongolia. In 1991–2003 almost two million Kazakhs are estimated to have left the country.

The migrants in Eastern Europe originated mostly from the CIS and Asia but also from other Eastern European countries. In Hungary, for example, estimates ranged between 40,000–150,000 undocumented migrants (Bade, 2003). In the Czech Republic they were estimated to be 100,000–140,000; the country also hosted Polish, Moldovan and Bulgarian migrants. Poland received migrants from Ukraine, Belarus and Russia, who were applying mostly for temporary rather than permanent residence permits, but also China, Vietnam and Armenia. It is estimated that a total of 100,000 undocumented migrants were detained at Ukraine's western border between 1991–2003 (Malynovska, 2004). The situation was similar for the Baltic States, even though slightly limited in size.

The example of Lithuania is telling. International migration was always present there, but transit migration only appeared in the 1990s. Being one of the better off parts of Eastern Europe, Lithuania up to the late 1980s and early 1990s was receiving a net annual inflow of 6000–8000 persons from the Soviet republics (Sipavicieno and Kanopiene, 1999). The country was also receiving migrants from Poland, Hungary and Czechoslovakia. This situation, however, soon changed, when transit migrants of CIS, Asian and African origin made their appearance creating a new type of flow. They never reached large proportions and still today few Asians go through Lithuania.

Transit migrants in Lithuania would usually be petty traders of two kinds; those that were planning to continue their journey to Germany and Poland, and those that wanted to trade in Lithuania. The first aimed for the Polish clothes markets and the German second-hand car market. They would also pick up unskilled work available here and there. They resorted to smugglers to cross the European borders. The second, usually Russians, Byelorussians and Ukrainians, would try to do petty trade in Lithuania, again for second-hand cars, clothes and other goods, mostly from China, Turkey and the UAE. They would use fake documents, even though most of the time they did not resort to smugglers and therefore they would try to organize the trip themselves. An ILO study found that both groups had contacts and networks in the country and were well informed about Lithuania prior to arrival (Sipavicieno and Kanopiene, 1999).

The case of traders was similar in Ukraine. 'Shuttle' traders were the most common form of labour migration. They brought in goods originating from countries like China and Turkey (Malynovska, 2004). According to an IOM study on transit migration in Ukraine in 1994, 26 per cent of migrants were doing trade between two or more countries, using Ukraine as a base, and they seemed quite satisfied with the living and working conditions in the country. Many of these 'shuttle' traders were Nigerian.

Transit migration would also take other forms. Studying, for example, was a common vector for migration in the 1990s. An IOM study on Russia (1994) estimated that 30 per cent of migrants arrived in Russia as students. Many among the Somalis living in Russia were graduates of Russian universities. As they were unable to renew their residence permits following graduation, they turned to UNHCR for assistance. Ten years later, studying is still used as a migration channel. As a result, many migrants in Russia are able to speak the language, irrespective of whether they plan to complete their studies or move on. The IOM study also concluded that some transit migrants were attracted by the developing asylum system in Russia at the time. Russia acceded to the 1951

Geneva Convention in 1993 and a year later 40,000 persons from Bangladesh, Iraq, Nepal and Somalia had applied for asylum.

As mentioned earlier, there was a tradition of Vietnamese and other Southeast Asian migration to Eastern Europe and the Soviet Union even back in the 1970s and 1980s. The transit flow of Asians and Africans increased considerably, however, during the 1990s. It is estimated that Moscow alone was hosting 250,000 migrants mostly from China and Sri Lanka in the mid-1990s, who were hoping to go to Western Europe. Another 150,000–300,000 transit migrants were estimated to be living in Belarus around the same time, most of whom were from Asia and the Middle East (Bade, 2003). The Asians found communities already established in the region that gave them support during the transit phase.

Being in transit in Eastern Europe and the former Soviet Union was a particularly difficult situation in the 1990s. Migrants from Afghanistan and Africa were the most vulnerable, as they seemed to be the target also of xenophobic sentiments. It is striking that, as the IOM study found, all Afghani and African migrants wanted to leave Russia as a result of this issue. A total of 70 per cent of migrants found the situation in Russia worse than expected. The factors affecting their decision to settle or move on were rather similar to those already mentioned in this book by other ethnic groups at different times. An additional factor affecting decision-making in Russia, in particular, is the question of distance – the distances the migrant had travelled so far in this vast country, and the distances he or she might need to cover for the next leg of the trip. And as also identified in other cases, the more financially independent the migrants were the easier they would move on – in other words, it was the poorest that would get 'stuck' in transit for longer (IOM Ukraine, 1994).

A similar IOM study in Poland (1994) distinguished between five types of transit migrants: the 'conscious or voluntary' migrants who saw migration as a way to improve their life and as an investment for the children; the 'accidental migrants' who had no defined plans or destination and travelled in groups; and the 'asylum seekers' that were often stranded in the country. There were also the 'return transit migrants', mostly Romanian rejected asylum seekers returned from Germany to Poland, and finally the 'transient residents', migrants awaiting opportunities who seemed more transient than permanent settlers. These observations share most of the characteristics identified in transit migration through Greece or through North African countries at present.

Managing migration was an issue still in its infancy in Eastern Europe and the CIS in the early 1990s. The first to work in this direction were the countries in Central and Eastern Europe with the prospect of EU accession. They were quick to adopt regulations and develop a framework in the style of other 'traditional' receiving countries. As we shall see in the next section, in many instances these developments were meant to create a policy framework from scratch. Following years of Soviet isolation, migration and asylum policy for the CIS was completely new; Russia had to create a legislative framework to deal with refugees and labour migrants, freedom of movement and migration to and from abroad, and develop a system of data collection (Heleniak, 2002).

On the contrary, the CIS did not feel the need or pressure to work in the direction of migration management – let alone asylum – until very late in the decade. It was the growth of irregular migration and increased interest on the side of European and accession countries that slowly brought migration onto the agenda.

6.2   The new migrations of the East

Transit in the new member states

Has migration to Eastern Europe increased because of EU accession? Around the time of accession, it was commonly argued that migration to or through Central and Eastern Europe was a result of the accession and was bound to increase after 2004. It is true that the Eastern enlargement of the EU in 2004 and 2007 changed the legal basis of cross-border movement and migration for these countries. However, according to Eurostat, migration to the new member states did not change dramatically the year after accession, compared to the previous years. Even in cases of a slight increase, this was still lower than numbers in the mid- and late 1990s.[1] At the same time, it is certain that migration management surfaced on the agenda as an important policy area as a result of the adoption of the EU acquis.

It is clear that the new member states had been destination countries for some time. Migrant communities had already settled in Poland by the 1990s. The peak of migrant smuggling and/or trafficking through Poland also happened in early to mid-1990s. In 1998 their number was estimated to be at least 30,000 annually (Iglicka and Weinar, 2006). The main groups were Ukrainian, Byelorussian and Russian. Hungary had been preoccupied with migration issues quite early as well. By 2002 there were 115,000 migrants with long-term residence permits in Hungary (Juhasz, 2003). The majority were migrants from neighbouring countries with Hungarian ethnicity; for example, Romanians of Hungarian origin, Ukrainians and other nationalities, including the Chinese. The Chinese had remained and settled in Hungary despite the introduction of visa requirements as of 1992.

The situation was also similar in the Czech Republic, which already had 252,000 registered migrants and another 300,000–350,000 undocumented prior to enlargement (Drbohlav, 2005). The majority of registered migrants came to the country for work or family reunion purposes, including Asians and nationals of the former Soviet Union. Evidence of the existence of migrant communities prior to enlargement are displayed by the regularization programmes conducted in Poland in 2003 that aimed to address the situation of 45,000–50,000 undocumented migrants (Iglicka, 2005). The Czech Republic has also been considering regularization for Ukrainians.

A reason for the growth of transit migrations via Eastern Europe back in the 1990s was the lack of an efficient migration policy framework. In addition, migration to these countries had a sense of experimentation at the time, a trial period that often took the form of frequent seasonal journeys, where migrants explored the channels, resources and prospects available. Living in Eastern Europe felt almost like being in the West, just a bit easier in terms of flexibility and informality in the labour market. It is striking that while 70 per cent of the migrants in Hungary had plans to migrate further, a quarter of them changed their plans (IOM Hungary, 1994). The more significant the participation in the labour market, the smaller their motivation was for further migration. The Czech labour market was also an important pull factor for migrants.

An important change for the new member states brought about by accession was the introduction of visa requirements to neighbours who previously would not have had any. Eastern Europeans were used to moving freely between countries, a policy which fostered solidarity and increased cross-border trade at the small and medium scale. Poland had now to request a visa from Belarus, Ukraine and Russia. Poland tried to strike a balance between applying visa requirements efficiently while at the same time preventing a barrier with its Eastern neighbours. The aim was to keep transborder traffic as regular as before enlargement and to some extent this was achieved (Iglicka and Weinar, 2006). In fact, the visas have been the main migration policy tool in Poland; the liberal visa regime applied to Ukraine serves almost as recruitment policy for Ukrainian labour, and so far it has managed to maintain immigration to the desired levels so as to meet labour needs.

In contrast, in Lithuania it seems that the introduction of visas has had the reverse effect, complicating relations and leading migrants to take the irregular path in order to cross to Lithuania. This is particularly the case for migrants coming from Belarus.

In the area of asylum, however, the changes brought about as a result of enlargement are more extensive, both in terms of refugee flows and in terms of the evolution of the asylum systems. The new member states had been asylum countries for some time. The Czech Republic, for example, hosted refugees from Yugoslavia, Ukraine, the former soviet Republics, and since 2000 refugees from Afghanistan, India and Romania. It is estimated that between 1999 and 2004, the country received 77,330 asylum seekers (Drbohlav, 2005). The number of applications in the Czech Republic, as also in Slovakia, Slovenia, Poland and Hungary, had already increased dramatically in 2003; every one of these countries received thousands of asylum seekers, in some cases twice as many as the year before. In 2004, the year of enlargement, and in 2005 the number of asylum applications remained equally high. A slight decrease was, however, observed in 2006.[2] Refugees in Eastern Europe have originated mostly from Russia (Chechen), but other nationalities are also represented.

It is worth noting that the number of applications in Eastern Europe was high even when the overall number of applications submitted in Europe decreased in 2005. The same trend was also observed in Greece for the same year. Another similarity between Greece and the new member states is the pressure created by the application of the Dublin regulation. These similarities stem from the fact that both cases are first asylum countries for refugees entering the European Union, and they are often seen as 'transit' countries. The question is whether asylum seekers actually stay in the new member states, or apply but then leave for Western Europe. It seems that most asylum applicants lodge an application, and then indeed leave for another member state: two-thirds of the 11,000 applications lodged in Slovakia in 2005 were terminated because applicants disappeared.[3] The same thing happened in Hungary – it is estimated that over 75 per cent of those who tried to leave the country illegally using smugglers were asylum seekers who had been residing in refugee camps (Juhasz, 2003). They were discouraged by the weak asylum system, the long procedures and the few chances for obtaining asylum. In other words, the asylum path has been used as a new common way of transiting through Eastern Europe.

More importantly, the accession process brought about a series of changes in policy-making and the conceptualization of migration and asylum in the new member states. Scholars have argued that the adoption of the acquis has essentially incorporated Eastern European countries into a restrictive refugee regime, already established among EU member states, turning them into gatekeepers for flows heading westwards (Lavenex, 1999). The countries' willingness to fight illegal migration and reduce the number of asylum seekers was used as a bargaining tool in exchange for membership. This is similar to the argument developed with regards to capacity building in North Africa.

On the other hand, some of these changes would have been necessary and inevitable, considering the demarcation of new borders and the growth of international migration in the region. EU conditionality came to close a gap that would in any case have existed because of objective political and social realities. One has to assess, however, both the positive and the negative aspects of these changes.

On the positive side, accession meant that certain minimum standards were now in place to improve the living conditions for migrant populations. The transposition of the EU directives on long-term residents, family reunion, residence permits for victims of trafficking and smuggling, and the admission of students for example brought about a series of changes affecting the lives of many migrants. Access to health care, the right to unite with one's family, protection and assistance to victims of trafficking, these are some of the new provisions made possible through the new policy framework. For some countries, like the Czech Republic, the long-term residence directive substantially reduced the waiting period from ten to five years.

The acquis also brought substantial changes in the area of asylum, introducing minimum standards for the reception of asylum seekers. The countries not only used to have different asylum traditions but also different understandings of the concept of 'refugees'. Poland, for example, distinguished between 'refugees' and 'forced migrants' and Hungary had provisions for 'convention' refugees, 'asylees' and 'refugees given shelter/ accepted refugees' (Juhasz, 2003). For years Hungary maintained a geographical limitation to refugees coming from Europe. This was lifted through the Asylum Act in 1998. The acquis also led to the development and improvement of refugee reception infrastructure.

Another positive development has been the general discourse and mobilization developed by civil society assisting migrants and refugees. Enlargement has been instrumental in this regard, either through accession funding or by stimulating a debate as a result of the reforms. Bulgaria, for example, which always had and still has only a small number of migrants and asylum seekers, has seen an impressive growth of civil society organizations providing assistance and advocating for the rights of migrant groups. In relation to that, the discourse on migration seems to have expanded towards other areas as well, including migrant rights, integration and admission.

On the other hand, EU accession has also created new burdens for the Eastern member states, particularly through the Dublin system that placed substantial responsibilities on their shoulders. Lavenex (1999) argues that the regime brought about by the acquis diffuses states' responsibilities by establishing a system of negative redistribution for the handling of asylum claims, in this way undermining the values of international refugee protection. At the same time, some new member states have also been more restrictive in granting asylum than they were before enlargement.[4] Furthermore, and despite policy developments and the building of reception infrastructure, asylum seekers living in the camps are no less vulnerable than before, or as observed in other European countries. Szczepaniková (2004), for example, mentions that asylum seekers in the Czech Republic live in the reception centres for months or years. While they were initially given the right to work, this right was lifted in 2002 as the number of applications started to increase. Without access to work, they experience a particularly vulnerable and marginalized situation.

Did policies essentially become stricter as a result of the accession? It is hard to say and this may differ from one country to another. Some countries may have had strict or perhaps stricter policies in certain areas before enlargement, and they may have become more liberal in some way. Other areas saw restrictions for the first time, like the introduction of visas to populations with which they previously had frequent interaction.

Another relevant question to ask is whether irregular and transit migration in particular has increased or decreased as a result of enlargement. It has been observed that as the date for accession was approaching, the number of irregular migrants apprehended at the borders dropped in certain countries. Enhanced border control was definitely a major step in this direction. Poland, for example, which had been working hard in this area, already saw transit number of irregular migrants dropping by 1998. The Polish borders are among the best guarded in Europe (Iglicka and Weinar, 2006). In contrast, the borders of the Czech and Slovak Republics seem to be more porous. Whether the flows of irregular migration actually decreased is not certain; it may be the case that migrants have been using smugglers and that border crossing has become more sophisticated. It may also be the case that more migrants enter legally and overstay their visas. Even though investing heavily on border control, Poland is also estimated to have 450,000 undocumented workers, most of whom have entered the country legally (Iglicka and Weinar, 2006). They may have overstayed their visas or they may be circulating back and forth to Ukraine, as practised for years before enlargement.

Transit in the Western Balkans

The Balkans are somewhere between the new member states and the neighbouring region of the CIS, in terms of migration flows to Europe and policy developments. Countries like Croatia and the Former Yugoslav Republic of Macedonia with a clear vision of accession have already entered the procedure of aligning their policies with EU standards. In Serbia, migration management is included in the negotiations for the Stabilization and Association Agreement with the European Union. Bosnia, which had over two million displaced after the war, half of whom were internally displaced, is still much preoccupied with the process of reconstruction and return of its Bosnian refugees. Yet, border management and the fight against trafficking also features centrally on the agenda. The situation in Kosovo is still too unstable to allow for advanced work in the area of migration management. The Union's overarching policy in the area is the stabilization and association process.

A part of irregular migration flows from Asia and Africa goes through the Balkans, particularly through Albania, Kosovo, the Former Yugoslav Republic of Macedonia, and Bosnia-Herzegovina. Transit migration in the Balkans is of limited scale, even though one finds all ethnic groups among them, including Asians and Africans (van Selm, 2007). Transit migration in the Balkans is also linked to past traditions of movement in the region and more or less follows the trails of smuggling and trafficking routes. Out of the estimated half-million irregular migrants who came to Europe in 2000, 50,000 of them went through the Balkans (Mavris, 2002). Certain conditions, such as the difficulty to control borders, corruption and conflicts in Kosovo, the Former Yugoslav Republic of Macedonia and Serbia had been strategically advantageous for the smuggling of migrants to Germany, Italy, Austria or Slovenia back in 2000–1. In former Yugoslavia, smugglers have always taken advantage of the unstable situation, the liberal visa regime and the absence of the rule of law, and transported people, cigarettes, alcohol, drugs and weapons.

Trafficking in the Balkans was vast in the late 1990s and may still be the most significant aspect of transit and irregular movements today; most countries have been source, transit and destination for trafficking practices. It was estimated that more than 6000 women from Bulgaria, Romania and Ukraine were trafficked to the Former Yugoslav Republic of Macedonia in only the first six months of 2000.[5] Albania was a key route in the trafficking of women from Moldova, Romania and Ukraine to Greece and Italy. It was even estimated that a large proportion of victims trafficked to Albania were men 'recruited' for begging or forced labour. In 2001 the United Nations mission in Bosnia closed 15 bars in Brcko where women from Eastern Europe were forced into prostitution.[6] The same phenomenon has been observed in Kosovo, where the international presence of UN and NATO has worked as a pull factor for trafficking for prostitution.

The Western Balkans have made substantial efforts to combat trafficking and to a large extent they have succeeded in raising awareness among girls about the risks involved with certain migration 'recruitment' agencies.

During the last few years and in the process of stabilization, the Western Balkans have worked to put in place a migration and asylum policy framework and a system of enhanced border surveillance. As in Eastern Europe, the visa regime seems to have worked as a main policy tool for migration management. Serbia has applied a stricter visa regime for Chinese citizens; Bosnia and Herzegovina has introduced a stricter visa regime for Turkish citizens at Sarajevo airport. On the other hand, the lack of a visa policy in Kosovo has prompted a significant number of illegal migrants to enter Europe directly via Prishtina airport. In September 2007, the Western Balkans also signed visa facilitation and readmission agreements with the European Union. The facilitation agreements simplify visas for businessmen, students and journalists, give multi-entry visas to frequent travellers and reduce the handling fees. The possibility of a visa-free regime is subject to discussion and linked to the overall progress that will be made in the area of border management and security.

Albania seems to be the only country in the Western Balkans that has developed a migration policy irrespective of EU accession prospects. Albania has been a major migrant-producing country, with over 900,000 Albanians living and working in Greece, Italy, the United States and Canada (Barjaba, 2004). After a large wave of uncontrolled emigration both in the early and then again in the late 1990s, emigration to Greece and Italy is now regulated by agreements and more legal due to the availability of legal migration channels. Albania has also been a transit country for migration flows crossing to Italy and Western Europe, even though smuggling and trafficking is now substantially reduced as a result of improvements in the policy framework.

The Western Balkans have also been active in intra-regional cooperation for migration and asylum and the return and reintegration of displaced persons. MARRI is one such initiative of regional ownership that is now part of the Southeast European Cooperation Process. One of the issues on MARRI's agenda is information exchange and cooperation to manage and decrease irregular transit migration.

Transit in the CIS

An undeniable result of enlargement has been the shifting of Europe's Eastern frontier further to the CIS and Central Asia. It is not certain whether migration flows increased after 2000 and notably, after EU enlargement, as these trends were already present in the region throughout the past decade. What is certain, however, is that more migrants have wanted to cross to Europe and, in view of a strict visa regime, enhanced border control, and informal labour possibilities they have been extending their stay in the CIS. In other words, migration flows have become increasingly more irregular and transient. As a result, border control, irregular migration and asylum have gradually gained significance and a place in the countries' policy-making agenda. Differences in policies and traditions, and a complicated visa regime among the CIS have only added to making migration management in the region a major challenge.

The CIS is not a homogeneous region and countries vary greatly in terms of population movements, labour markets, policy regimes and challenges. Russia is one of the major destination countries in the world. Besides the sheer size of its labour market, the relatively better state of Russia's social and economic situation compared to many of its neighbours; the emigration of its own nationals, particularly highly skilled, and consequent growing need for labour count as decisive factors in that respect (Ivakhniouk, 2006; Voronina, 2006). The fact that many of those non-Russian nationals speak Russian makes the Russian Federation a particularly attractive destination (Patzwald, 2004). Half of the country's labour migrants are nationals of other countries in the CIS and the rest are from South and Southeast Asia. The Chinese are supposed to be close to five million.[7] The number of migrants from Iraq, Iran and Afghanistan is estimated at 500,000 to one million (Bade, 2003).

The country is also a popular transit space because it offers improved transport connections and ease of access to the West, for example for those migrants that manage to obtain a residence permit. The number of irregular migrants is estimated to be vast, ranging from five to ten million (Voronina, 2006). Other estimates put the number at 3.5 million.[8] In the 1990s it was estimated that Russia was also hosting about one million draft evaders from the Caucasus (IOM Russia, 1994). Russia has now signed bilateral agreements with all CIS countries to regulate labour migration. In an effort to combat the informal economy, Russia passed a law in April 2007 restricting work in the street markets for non-Russian nationals; it is estimated that the number of vendors, many of them Tajiks, dropped by 40 per cent.[9]

Kazakhstan is another major destination and transit country in the region. Kazakhstan receives labour migrants from neighbouring countries, mostly Uzbekistan and Kyrgyzstan. They usually take up low-skilled and low-paid jobs that locals are unwilling to take. Buldekbaev (2006) mentions that every year an estimated one million migrants come to Kazakhstan for seasonal work, many of them regularly and through guest worker programmes. The country has now established labour quotas to cover these needs. In 2006 Kazakhstan also developed a law on regularizing and taxing irregular migrants. Communities of Afghan and Pakistani migrants are settled in the country. Belarus also hosts large numbers of irregular migrants, estimated to be close to 100,000. They originate from China, Vietnam, Afghanistan, Pakistan, Iran, Iraq and India. In fact, it is the same ethnic groups that have been migrating to Eastern Europe during the last ten years, only bigger in size. In Ukraine an average of 25,000–28,000 undocumented migrants are identified annually through internal controls (Malynovska, 2006. The other transit countries also display some destination characteristics, even though their labour markets do not sustain migrant labour.

Smuggling practices in the former Soviet republics may in principle not differ from the ones described in North Africa and in Greece/ Turkey, nevertheless a number of additional factors suggest that smuggling here is of much larger scale and frequently overlapping with other types of smuggling or human trafficking (IOM, 2006). This can be attributed to the large distances and geographical areas that require a larger network involving more people and greater coverage. It also has to do with past traditions of smuggling in the region as a common way to trade goods across borders and an extensive operation of human trafficking which is omnipresent, making it almost impossible to avoid traffickers.

Futo and colleagues (2005) found that smugglers are part of large networks that are very organized, very hierarchical and with clear division of labour (including roles such as 'recruiters', 'organizers', 'consigners', 'drivers', 'guides', etc.). It is only the lowest level in the pyramid that operates near the borders. According to them, the prices from China to Europe are somewhere between 10,000–15,000 USD, from Pakistan and India 8000 USD, from Afghanistan to Europe somewhere around 4000–6000 USD. It is still 2000–3000 USD to cross to Europe from Moldova and over 5000 USD to cross from Ukraine. Migrants tend to prefer passports of countries that do not require a visa for Western Europe.

There are many routes to follow from Asia to Europe, and almost all of them pass from some Central Asian, former Soviet republic. The Black Sea region is central to the configuration of the migration routes: the routes are separated between those going through Turkey or the Balkans, those going through Eastern Europe and the new member states, and those going through the Baltic States.

The Asians that can afford it fly directly to Moscow. For the rest, common routes are through the Russian–Mongolian or Russian–Chinese border, or more commonly via Kazakhstan. For this, migrants arrive first in Tajikistan, Uzbekistan and Kyrgyzstan by car or on foot, and then travel further with the help of smugglers through Kazakhstan and Russia. They enter Kyrgyzstan with visas they have obtained in Kyrgyz or other embassies abroad. The visas are valid and usually obtained for tourism, study or business. Bangladeshis and Pakistanis register as students in private establishments in Kyrgyzstan. Migrants may then obtain fake passports from Kyrgyzstan. Kyrgyz passports are also known to be used by Uyghur separatists. The Fergana Valley spreading across Uzbekistan, Tajikistan and Kyrgyzstan is particularly open to movements of people and goods in various directions. Afghan refugees often tend to go via Turkmenistan or Uzbekistan.

The size of the Russian–Kazak border (over twice the length of that between Mexico and the USA) makes it very hard to control and is a popular crossing. Pakistani and Bangladeshi migrants also use the route through Kazakhstan. According to an IOM study (2006) in Kazakhstan, they may take the following routes: from Dhaka to Delhi in India by train, then by car to Tajikistan, to Kyrgyzstan, and then to Kazakhstan. There is also another route for Bangladeshis by train to Bombay, then by plane to Dubai, then to an African country and from there to Europe, as described in Chapter 5. There is also the land route via Tajikistan and Dubai, which follows the trafficking trails.

There is also the route via Azerbaijan; migrants enter through the border with Iran or through the Caspian Sea. A common route for Iraqis is Iraq–Iran–Azerbaijan–Europe. Around 80 per cent are smuggled through the border with Turkey and Georgia, walking or hiding in trucks. An IOM study in 2003 found that most transit migrants were Afghan, Pakistani, Iranian and Iraqi. Many enter the country legally, the rest use fake passports. Popular destinations are Greece, the Netherlands, Norway, the United Kingdom and France (Aliyev, 2006). Indians and Pakistani also use the route via Azerbaijan to Russia and then to Europe; according to an ICMPD (2005) study, this is facilitated by 'travel agencies' in Baku.

Another route is through Armenia, which seems to have become more popular after 2002, as economic growth provides opportunities for local temporary employment. Georgia generally does not seem to be a transit country, not as much as Azerbaijan where much of the trafficking and smuggling networks are concentrated; there is, however, some transit migration of Asians and Africans going to Russia, Ukraine or the Middle East. In 2002–3, Georgia received transit Kurds from Iraq.

Just like in North Africa, the locals also follow the same routes: Uzbeks, Tajiks, Turkmen and Kyrgyz all join in the routes of the Asians, even though they may not resort to smuggling as much as the South/Southeast Asians. Rather they may try to apply for refugee status in other CIS countries or in Eastern and Western Europe directly. Alternatively, they enter another CIS country legally and then overstay.

Once in Kazakhstan or in Russia, almost all migrant groups take a break. They spend a substantial amount of time ranging from a few months to one or two years and often move between different cities. Those that have the resources and energy move on to Europe. That's particularly the case for the Southeast Asians; many CIS nationals, however, will prefer to stay in the CIS republics.

Crossing from Russia, many take the route through Ukraine and to Belarus, both major entry points to Poland. The border between Russia and Belarus is open, which makes entry easy. This is not the case, however, with the other Byelorussian borders; the result being that migrants get 'stuck' in Belarus. Smugglers operate extensively in the country; they even set up fake companies to 'invite' migrant employees. Migrants spend some time in Belarus, most commonly by overstaying their visas, before they try to continue westwards. They often register as students. UNHCR estimates that up to 15,000 – 20,000 illegal migrants are in Belarus every year, including 15-20 per cent who are possibly in need of international protection.[10] Others go through Moldova, and then enter illegally into the Czech Republic, Hungary and Greece, or into Germany and Austria. This is, for example, a common route for Armenians. The lack of control over Moldova's external border in Transnistria means that about 200 km of border remain open (Jandl, 2003).

The main destination countries for CIS nationals are Germany, Greece, Spain, Portugal, the Netherlands and the Middle East. At the same time, demographic challenges and the sheer size of labour markets make Russia and Kazakhstan equally attractive destinations. It is also the fact that as easy as migrants find it to enter Russia and Kazakhstan, so also is it as hard to exit with the result that they get 'stuck' in the country and settle permanently. Ivakhniouk (2004) mentions that there is an estimated 300,000 transit migrants from Afghanistan, China, Angola, Pakistan, India, Sri Lanka, Turkey and Ethiopia that are now 'stuck' in Russia.

According to studies on irregular and transit migration in the CIS, being in transit in this region is no different than the situation observed in Morocco or Greece. Migrants and refugees work in day jobs in the informal economy and try to collect money for the next leg of the trip. Most studies, however, point out the fact that migrants increasingly engage in criminal activities as well, be it petty trade, trafficking or drug smuggling.

Transit migrants tend to avoid seeking help from the authorities or local NGOs, out of fear of deportation. Local and transnational networks and smuggling contacts seem to provide a space for socialization and support. According to Ivakhniouk's (2006) research in Russia, transit migrants do not engage in relations with locals. Some stay in detention centres and reception camps, others share accommodation with friends in the city. Those staying in refugee camps may end up living there for months or even years, as observed also in detention centres in Ukraine.[11] It has been observed that migrants who had been returned to their country of origin often emigrated again, going to the same country as before.

It seems migrants are not informed about the conditions and prospects of living and working in Europe when leaving their country. Yeganyan (2006) observes that people attempt to reach Western Europe thinking that there will be no visa or other requirements and that they will have access to work. They are also motivated by false advertisements circulated by local 'travel agencies' who promise migration possibilities in Europe.

Moreover, the issue of internally displaced populations and refugees from neighbouring former Soviet republics is a long-standing policy issue. Most of these cases are protracted refugee situations, for example in Armenia, Tajikistan, Turkmenistan, Azerbaijan, and Georgia. Most refugees in Georgia are Internally Displaced Persons (IDPs) and Chechens from Russia. There are also Georgian refugees seeking asylum in other CIS countries and in Eastern Europe. Kazakhstan has also received Chechen, Tajik, Afghan and Chinese Uyghur refugees. Azerbaijan hosts hundreds of thousands of IDPs, as well as Azerbaijanis from Armenia following the Nagorno–Karabagh conflict, and Meshketian Turks.

In contrast, asylum seekers from third countries outside the former Soviet Union have only recently made their appearance in large numbers in the CIS. Few of them apply for asylum; one can assume with a degree of certainty that they remain undocumented and wait to apply once in Western Europe. For example, in Azerbaijan refugees from Iraq, Afghanistan, Turkey and Russia prefer not to lodge an application for fear of being returned to their country of origin; only 10–15 per cent of irregulars are estimated to lodge an application (Aliyev, 2006). In the Western CIS, the asylum seekers are slightly greater in number; an average of 1200–1400 foreigners apply for asylum in Ukraine annually (Malynovska, 2006). At the end of 2000 Russia hosted 667,000 registered 'refugees' and 'forced migrants' from other former Soviet republics (most of which were Chechen), and only 9710 refugees originating from third countries (Heleniak, 2002).

Thus asylum for third-country nationals is a new challenge. Some countries, like Russia and Ukraine, had already acceded to the 1951 Convention back in the mid-1990s, others have done so only recently. Russia, Belarus and Ukraine now host asylum seekers from Afghanistan, Africa and Asia. In Moldova, most refugees are Chechens from Russia. In all three countries, refugees live predominantly in urban areas and particularly in the capital cities. The asylum systems and reception infrastructure are still weak. In Russia, for example, the three reception centres for third-country nationals are not sufficient to meet the needs of the population. None of them is located in Moscow, where most asylum seekers are residing. Asylum seekers also have no access to work, which in Russia is a significant handicap to their survival.[12] A visit by Human Rights Watch in Ukraine, for instance, found substandard conditions of detention, physical abuse, verbal harassment and severe overcrowding. It was also reported that migrants were being returned by Ukraine to countries where they could face risks.[13] In the absence of an asylum policy in the CIS countries up to a few years ago, UNHCR and other international organizations cater for the refugees and promote resettlement.

Border management has been a major challenge in the region for over 15 years now. First of all is the question of border demarcation, which in some cases was completed very recently; Lithuania and Latvia completed the demarcation of their border in 2004, with Kazakhstan finalizing the demarcation of its border with Uzbekistan and Kyrgyzstan even more recently. Defining the border line still remains a challenge in certain areas, despite the signing of international agreements. The Moldovan border seems to suffer from such problems. Some borders are more permeable than others, as, for example, the open border between Belarus and Russia. The border between Ukraine and Russia also seems to witness a lot of traffic and crossings. In Georgia, the only clearly marked and controlled border is the one with Turkey. Another important factor to take into account in the drawing and management of borders are the bilateral and internal ethnic conflicts.

Another issue has been the lack of infrastructure and resources for border management. Belarus, for instance, had some difficulties in implementing return operations because of lack of both financial resources and detention centres. Armenia is known to have recruited Russian guards to control its borders with Iran and Turkey (ICMPD, 2005).

Linked to this is the effect of the complicated visa regime among the CIS. In October 1992 the 12 CIS countries signed an agreement for visa-free movement of their citizens (known as the 'Bishkek agreement'). Only a few years later, however, in 1999 Turkmenistan withdrew from the agreement, followed by Uzbekistan in 2000. In turn, Russia, Belarus, Kazakhstan, Kyrgyzstan and Tajikistan tried to give a second opportunity to a visa-free regime and created the 'Eurasian Economic Community' in 2000, reinforced by a protocol to the agreement in 2005. On top of this, countries moved into signing bilateral visa agreements, such as that between Uzbekistan and Kyrgyzstan. As a result, the visa regime in the region is now complex and rather difficult to monitor. In fact, behind the routes of transit migration one could see the threads of visa-free regimes as operating at a particular time. For example, up to 2005 Georgians would be required to have a visa for Russia, but no visa for Belarus; hence they entered Russia through Belarus. This visa-free regime was abolished in 2005, and as a result they had to look for alternative routes.

In this context border management is a challenge with political and military significance beyond migration management, and has become a central topic in international cooperation projects. Through European and other international funding during the early years of this decade a number of initiatives have taken place to support border control capacity, provide training, equipment, and exchange of knowledge and information. IOM, ICMPD and OSCE have been important players in this area.

Aside from border management, the CIS countries have also shown interest in the management of migration flows. Partly responding to European pressures for migration control but also, more importantly, responding to their own pressures and the need to control and manage this new phenomenon, the CIS have recently embarked on the development of a migration policy framework and the regulation of labour migration to their territories. Practices are still scattered and work needs to be done to make efforts more concentrated; progress is still lagging behind in a number of areas, as for example in technical infrastructure for registration of migrants, document security, readmission agreements, and the fight against corruption that is still widespread. Some of the new member states have offered to provide technical assistance and knowledge transfer in designing administrative structures and drafting the national legislation, particularly in areas such as refugee protection, return, the setting up of reception centres, visa policies and readmission agreements.

A level of intra-regional cooperation has also started to develop in this area. The CIS countries have developed an Agreement on Cooperation of CIS Member States in Combating Illegal Migration, signed on 6 March 1998 by all countries except Turkmenistan; the agreement remained dormant until 2004, when the first meeting took place and established a framework for cooperation on issues such as border control, deportations, exchange of information and training.

They have also established bilateral and regional platforms of collaboration with their counterparts who are mostly affected; Russia, for example, works closely with Belarus; Belarus works with Russia and Ukraine, but also with Poland, Latvia and Lithuania as it has an interest in a more Baltic grouping. Armenia cooperates with Georgia and Uzbekistan. Ukraine has signed bilateral agreements with CIS and other countries where Ukrainians are residing. Then there is the level of regional cross-border cooperation; usually activities are in the area of information exchange, knowledge transfer and capacity building. A regional CIS conference on refugees and other forms of displaced persons was convened in 1996 bringing together IOM, UNHCR and OSCE. Its Programme of Action served as a blueprint for interventions in the region for the period 1996–2000. A follow-up to the CIS conference was initiated for the period 2000–4.

The Soderkoping process is an inter-agency initiative launched in 2001 and lead by the UNHCR, the European Commission and the Swedish Migration Board to foster cross border cooperation on migration and asylum between EU member states on the one side, and Ukraine, Belarus and Moldova on the other. The Process provides support for capacity building and awareness raising for asylum among government and senior officials.

Another intergovernmental initiative has been the 'redirection' of the Budapest process towards the CIS as of 2004, financed by the EC and supported by old and new member states, including Poland and the Czech Republic. There are also various AENEAS, ARGO and TACIS-funded projects in Central Asia around the issue of border control and management.

All CIS have signed and ratified the UN Smuggling and Trafficking Protocols, none of them, however, considers smuggling of migrants as a legal offence in its national legislation. On the contrary, an area that has seen a great proliferation of policy measures has been the combat of human trafficking. Human trafficking for prostitution or forced labour has been vast in the CIS for the last 15 years and up to the present; women have been 'recruited' and trafficked to UAE, Turkey, Pakistan and Europe for prostitution; men are also being trafficked to Russia and Turkey for forced labour; and children are trafficked for begging. Kazakhstan and Kyrgyzstan are at the same time source, transit and destination countries for trafficking, even internally from rural to urban areas (IOM, 2006). A case came out in 2004 of children trafficked from orphanages in Azerbaijan for the purpose of selling their organs.[14]

Various international collaborations and conferences have taken place over the last few years, training curricula have been developed for enforcement officers and structures and organizations have been set up to deal with the phenomenon. Belarus, for example, a major source country, has signed agreements of collaboration with Russia, Ukraine, Poland and Turkey, and has initiated a state programme to combat trafficking. Moldova, still considered Number One source country for trafficking to the Balkans and Western Europe, has also made substantial efforts.

As we saw in Chapter 2, the CIS cooperate with the European Union in the framework of association agreements, the ENP and the TACIS programmes. Readmission agreements feature centrally on the agenda.

The Western CIS seem to have the same concerns as the North African neighbours, namely the fear that they may become a magnet for irregular migration as a result of Europe's restrictive policies. They have been vocal in asking for more funding and support, as well as visa facilitation. Ukraine, indeed, gained visa facilitation in June 2007, together with the readmission agreement that was signed on the same day. Regarding readmission agreements, it is true that up to recently, the CIS were not particularly targeted as part of the Union's readmission policy. Today, the Partnership and Cooperation Agreements with all countries include a clause on readmission with the EC, as well as the commitment on the countries' side to conclude bilateral agreements with member states. Most CIS also have bilateral agreements in place with certain member states.

In addition, the recent Global Approach to migration has lately been expanded to include the Union's eastern and southeastern neighbours. The concepts of 'migration profiles' and 'cooperation platforms' are potentially applicable to the Caucasus and Central Asia, in the sense of mainstreaming migration in these countries' external relations and development cooperation with the European Union. Capacity building will continue to be a core component for border management, law enforcement and intra-regional cooperation.

The present chapter has presented the history and current profile of transit migration and migration management in Europe's eastern neighbours. Transit migration was a dominant mobility pattern in the Eastern bloc and remained even after the disintegration of the Soviet Union. The drawing of external borders and the introduction of visas within a fortnight turned internal transient movements into international – and often irregular – movements. Today, the Caucasus and Central Asia is Europe's new eastern border and a transit region par excellence. The CIS countries face a complex set of migration movements and challenges, from the emigration of their own nationals, to intra-regional ethnic migration, to temporary 'shuttle' migration, to forced displacement internally and across borders. For countries with large populations working abroad, like Georgia, Ukraine, Moldova and Albania, capitalizing on their diaspora and protecting the rights of their nationals is a primary concern. Border management is a policy area that poses major challenges because of the lack of infrastructure, the length of the countries' borders and, in some cases also, territorial disputes. Human trafficking has been a significant social problem affecting all CIS, Eastern European and Western Balkan countries for over a decade. Smuggling practices are long established and part of informal and regular crossings of people and goods across borders that to a large extent were previously internal borders. The tradition of transit movements in the region is sustained also by informal economic practices, as is the case in Russia, Kazakhstan and Ukraine. To some extent, transit migrants in Russia or Ukraine are better off than the transit migrants in North Africa presented in the previous chapter, because they can support their livelihoods in the informal economy. On the other hand, transit refugees in need of protection are as vulnerable as elsewhere in transit regions, because they lack the safeguards for access to, and delivery of, protection, access to employment and durable solutions. With the exception of those lucky enough to be resettled, the rest find themselves stranded in this vast transit space for years.

7
Conclusion

This study has focused on the phenomenon of transit migration as experienced inside and outside EU borders. It has presented the case both from a top-down and a bottom-up perspective, namely the perspective of the transit countries and that of the migrants themselves. I have used three different case studies to illustrate the transit experience: the case of member states on the periphery of the Union, exemplified by Greece; the case of Europe's southern neighbours, exemplified by the Maghreb countries; and the case of Eastern European and CIS countries bordering the EU in the East.

Transit migration has been defined as the time between emigration and settlement that may or may not develop into further migration, depending on a number of structural and individual factors. The analysis has shown that the outcome of this process is affected as much by social and policy structures as it is by social networks and other individual factors. Emotions, preferences and physical condition can have as much of an impact as policy frameworks and decisions. Transit migration is characterized by ambiguity and rarely follows set plans. It is hard to predict its outcome. This makes it difficult to measure and quantify, or develop effective policy responses.

Transit migration is not a new or separate migrant category, but rather a process that cuts across various categories: irregular migrants, asylum seekers, refugees, regularized migrants and trafficked persons may all find themselves in transit at some point. Irregular migrants and asylum seekers become mixed in migration flows during that phase. It is common for refugees to remain undocumented in the transit countries for years, or to apply for asylum and yet leave for another country in the future. Transit migration is not, however, synonymous with irregular migration. It is possible that lawfully resident migrants and asylum seekers stay in transit and move to another country whenever the opportunities arise, or on the contrary, that an illegal migrant is neither planning nor willing to leave the host country. All this makes it particularly difficult to address transit migration, especially considering that most countries and policy-making bodies tend to approach migrants through rigid dichotomies, such as forced versus voluntary, legal versus illegal, newcomers versus settled migrants.

Social ties, family and friends at home or in other countries, and relations with locals are all instrumental during the transit phase. Local ties, in particular, often create a 'support structure' that provides an environment for mobilization in the transit country. Transit migrants follow surprising and often unexpected routes, and spend substantial amounts of time in more than one country before they eventually settle somewhere. Being in transit is a condition of increased vulnerability, characterized by poverty, semi-protection, insecurity and social exclusion. This is an important point that usually remains neglected in the migration literature. Refugees, in particular, are the most vulnerable among migrants in transit, as they lack access to, and adequate standards of, protection while in transit. This vulnerability makes it imperative to address transit migration irrespective of location, whether inside or outside European borders.

Studies from the mid-1990s in Eastern Europe indicate that transit migration is not as new as it is usually presented. Transient movements are an integral part of past mobility and trade routes across various regions, cutting through both internal and external borders. The difference is that today transit migrations are more irregular, politicized and securitized. The perilous journeys that migrants take and the numbers of victims at Europe's land borders and seashores are what has brought the issue to the forefront. In addition, the emphasis that the EU now places on migration management and cooperation with third countries has further contributed to attracting public attention to the issue.

Transit migration is often neglected by states because of the assumption that migrants will soon leave the country. This study has shown that the transit phase in a given country can, in fact, last for years. The explicit or implicit argument about the temporariness of transit migration becomes, then, just another excuse for both the reluctance to accept the reality of migration and the failure to develop an efficient policy framework. An additional obstacle is the widespread failure of states to grasp the truly regional dimension of transit migration and the impact it has on more than one country.

This study has shown that transit migration is not only happening in third countries but also in the Unions' member states. Greece was presented as a country that occupies both a destination and transit position. While usually not in the centre of attention in migration debates and policies in the Mediterranean, Greece in fact receives substantial migration flows from the east and south. A strong informal economy and a weak migration policy framework allow for sustained irregularity. The current asylum system is weak and unpromising, characterized by extremely low recognition rates, lack of proper reception infrastructure, and frequent detention and deportation practices. As a result, refugees may apply for asylum in Greece only in order to have access to the formal labour market and health care. Others will remain undocumented, hoping to seek asylum in another member state in the future. Some of the refugees leave the country after a while, yet there are many that stay for a number of years. In fact, this policy of restriction and neglect does not necessarily lead to a decrease in refugee flows. It is worth noting that despite this policy approach, in 2007 Greece was the third most popular destination country for refugees in the industrialized world.

Part of the problem in Greece, as in other countries of the EU periphery, is the unfair burden placed on them as a result of the Dublin system. This is of course even more true of certain new member states, particularly Cyprus and Malta. That system requires them to shoulder a disproportionate number of asylum seekers purely because they happen to be land or sea entry points to Europe. This being said, another part of the problem in Greece and many of these other countries is local mismanagement and lack of political will to prioritize migration policy, seek funds, develop infrastructure and consolidate a framework for asylum and migration that meets adequate standards. In relation to this, 'transit' is usually presented as a purely short-term state, and therefore as an excuse for the lack of adequate development. This policy attitude finds its roots back in the years 1996–9 at a time when the country was completely unfamiliar with, and unprepared to face, situations of mass refugee arrivals. Ten years and thousands of refugee arrivals later, the Greek reception policy (and attitude) is no different.

Transit migration is experienced in a similar fashion on the outside of European borders, even though problems may be more acute in this case because the neighbouring countries are lagging behind in terms of social and economic development. The North African countries are now origin, transit and destination countries all at the same time. It should be noted that two-thirds of the migrants crossing illegally from North Africa to Europe are, in fact, locals from the Maghreb – a reminder of the direct correlation between development and emigration. More generally, the phenomenon of migration is not new in the area. There is a history of trans-Saharan movements and some current migration routes follow old trade and migration routes on the continent. All these flows to and through the region have increased substantially in recent years as a result of structural factors, such as infrastructure development and technologies that make crossing of the borders easier and faster. In this context, the policies developed internally in the EU have a direct impact on realities in the Maghreb. The more difficult it becomes for migrants and refugees to arrive in Europe, the more transit migration increases in North Africa. In addition, distinguishing between economic migrants and refugees becomes particularly difficult. The lack of proper asylum procedures remains the fundamental problem in that context.

North African countries are both unprepared and unwilling to develop a fully fledged migration and asylum policy, out of fear that this might serve as a pull factor for more migrant arrivals. This policy of neglect does not, however, seem to pay off in reducing migration flows any more than the similar approach has done in Greece. Instead, migrants and refugees end up staying in North Africa for months or even years irrespective of policies in force in the country.

The policy frameworks for migration and asylum differ from one North African country to another, but it is possible to identify a number of common characteristics. All countries maintain a restrictive approach, lack the necessary infrastructure and resources, resort regularly to arrests and deportation as a way to alleviate the problem, and they all lack a proper system for asylum. Labour markets also display some similarities, even though it seems that in certain countries migrants can survive through occasional jobs in the informal economy while in others this is much harder. Sub-Saharan Africans have been migrating, for example, for work in Libya for some years now. On the other hand, Morocco – itself a developing country with high poverty rates – does not seem to offer many work opportunities. Migrants and asylum seekers tend to rely here on NGO assistance for their survival. Refugees in transit are perhaps the most vulnerable cases as protection standards are low, the opportunities for durable solutions few and the risk of *refoulement* permanent. For most refugees, the way out is to spend some time in North Africa and try to cross to Europe illegally. Not all of them succeed in this, however, and many, in fact, end up staying in North Africa.

Transit migration also reaches large proportions in Eastern Europe and the CIS countries. Nevertheless, the issue does not seem to be received with the same level of alarm by Europeans and locals as in North Africa. This may be because border crossings here do not result in as many human tragedies as in the Mediterranean, and therefore are not as mediatized. It may also be because Eastern European and Central Asian countries have a history of cross-border movements dating from before the collapse of the Soviet Union. Many of these past movements were transient, and people used informal labour practices to work and stay in different countries, for example as suitcase traders or other workers. Smuggling routes were long established, transporting people, goods, drugs and arms. The disintegration of the Soviet Union and the drawing of new international borders brought about considerable changes in political balances, population composition and cross-border movements. As internal borders became international, emigration and immigration became to a large extent irregular. Central and Eastern Europe were transformed into popular transit countries for migrants from the Caucasus, Central and East Asia during the 1990s. The CIS countries saw large-scale emigration of their own nationals and transit migration of Asians trying to reach the West.

The new member states of Central and Eastern Europe soon entered a phase of reforms in the process of adopting the EU acquis. Today they continue to be destination countries for certain communities from the CIS and Asia, even though enlargement has not had any sizeable direct effect on economic migration. On the contrary, the number of asylum seekers reaching Eastern Europe boomed the year of enlargement and the years that followed. The Eastern European member states are similar to Greece insofar as many asylum seekers register in the country but remain in transit, and often leave for a Western EU member state a few years later. On the other hand, they are also different in that they are not as popular destination countries for economic migrants as Greece. The Western Balkans are quite close to the new member states in terms of policy reforms, even though they receive only limited migration flows and are still preoccupied with fundamental local issues, such as post-war return, reintegration, and related population and minority issues. But, a central policy issue that has affected all countries in Eastern Europe, the Western Balkans and the CIS in recent years is large-scale human trafficking.

Today the Caucasus and Central Asia is the Eastern transit region par excellence. Migrants and refugees may spend a long time in transit and work in the informal economy, until the conditions (financial, networks or other) allow them to move further westwards. Distances are enormous and the time spent in transit may be longer than observed elsewhere. Certain countries like Russia and Kazakhstan have developed into proper destination countries and accommodate thousands and, some say, millions of undocumented migrants who live as invisibles and work in the country. The CIS countries have only recently started to develop a framework for migration and asylum policy. The complexity of the migration flows and visa regulations, but also the unresolved issues of territorial dispute and the resulting high number of internally displaced persons, make migration management in this region particularly challenging.

The policy of the European Union in the area of migration and asylum is directly related to the management of transit migration in the neighbouring regions. An efficient and robust policy framework that gives migrants possibilities of entry and work in various sectors, and refugees access to protection in a harmonized way across the Union, would diminish many of the reasons that push people to live as undocumented in transit. However, the European Union still has to go a long way to reach this goal, and a truly common policy is not likely to see the light until after 2010. Migration policies remain largely national policies. The divergence between member states in terms of standards, rights and procedures is still significant. A policy of admissions for low-skilled and unskilled labour would be a major step forward, but no agreement between member states seems forthcoming so far. Cooperation in the effort to combat irregular migration is more intensive and concrete, nevertheless it will not be sustainable if it is not coordinated with a labour migration and asylum policy.

Until now a substantial part of the policy work has focused on the area of border surveillance, control and operational support to member states and third countries. But the fight against irregularity is not only about preventing people from entering the continent illegally, it is also about combating illegal hiring. The issue is now on the table and it remains to be seen in what form and with what sanctions it will be implemented at national level. In addition, migration control seems to lack some essential safeguards to support refugee protection and the protection of the fundamental rights of irregular migrants.

In the area of asylum, a number of important steps have been taken during the last five years. The union currently finds itself at a crossroads. Asylum legislation and implementation are being reviewed and evaluated, and new ideas are being put forward about the future EU asylum policy. A number of weaknesses and difficulties suggest important parts of the current system would need re-thinking. The way responsibilities for asylum processing are being allocated between member states is, for example, clearly problematic in that it places an unjustified burden on the Union's peripheral countries. Likewise, the EU needs to develop ways to ensure that member states comply with certain minimum standards. Indeed, criteria for granting refugee status, asylum procedures, reception conditions and the quality of protection delivered still differ widely among member states.

More importantly, Europe needs to remain engaged in refugee protection and promote protection as its guiding principle. Civil society and refugee protection organizations often refer to 'the spirit of Tampere', as an emblematic approach that managed to balance between migration management and protection responsibilities. Tampere contained, indeed, some ideas that were visionary in their time. The next step would be for Europe to develop an asylum policy approach in which the quality of the asylum it delivers is the priority – not the focus on how to prevent people from lodging an application in Europe. A practical and feasible first step could be for the European countries to engage more in resettlement in order to prove their commitment to refugee protection in practice.

During the last couple of years, a new stream in migration and asylum policy has developed, mainstreaming migration in the Union's overall foreign and development policy with third countries. Previously, migration was approached as a home affairs issue, from the perspective of receiving countries. The link between migrant arrivals in Europe and push factors, the conditions in origin and transit countries, or the impact of the EU's development policy were rarely made explicit. Now, according to the newly conceived 'global approach to migration', the issue will be directly related to development, for example through projects in the transit and origin countries that aim to support local employment, training and possibilities for legal migration to Europe, circular and temporary migration schemes, or the contribution of diasporas to development. Migration management will feature centrally in many aspects of development policy, from social and political development, to good governance, human rights and security. Considering that migration is by definition a cross-cutting issue integrated in numerous policy areas, this comprehensive approach could be welcomed as a positive, constructive and pragmatic step.

This book's analysis ties in with recent policy trends in the external dimension of migration and the 'global approach to migration'. It shows that transit countries are lagging behind in terms of capacities to manage migration and provide protection to refugees found in their territories. Substantial work and support is needed in order for countries to reach standards and capacities to effectively address the various challenges. All transit countries have a responsibility to deliver protection to refugees and safeguard the fundamental rights of all migrants found in their territory irrespective of status. The right to asylum in the transit countries should not be treated as an immigration 'threat' but as a fundamental right, enshrined in the Universal Declaration on Human Rights and the relevant international instruments that the countries have signed and ratified. Delivering protection should remain a goal and not a burden. In addition, efforts to build asylum systems in the transit and origin countries need to be synchronized with other measures giving solutions to the presence of irregular migrants. Otherwise, the asylum system risks being abused by most illegally resident migrants.

Irrespective of where it occurs, transit migration poses particular challenges to the individuals involved. The uncertainty and vulnerability involved greatly adds to the feeling of insecurity. On the one hand, it does not allow migrants to completely rebuild their lives in a country that is likely to be only a place of temporary stay. On the other hand, since the country is just as likely to become a place of lengthy or permanent settlement, the individual tries to develop ties and seek the conditions that will allow him to integrate. Being neither here nor there, the transit migrant lives in a permanent state of limbo and instability.

Besides the strains it can put on individuals, transit migration also poses particular challenges to the states involved. The ambiguities of transit migration make it particularly difficult to develop adequate policy responses. Put simply, it is much more difficult to develop policy measures for a population that may or may not settle, than for a population that falls clearly into one of those categories. Furthermore, the extent to which a country is affected by transit migration depends not only on its own policies, but also on the policies developed by other countries. We have seen this chain impact both within the EU, and outside its borders. Ultimately, transit migration is a global phenomenon that needs common policy responses.

Today, managing migration flows remains a major challenge globally, affecting origin, transit and destination countries. This is partly due to the sheer size and complexity of international population movements in the era of globalization. It is also due to the increasing irregularity in border crossings, migrant stay and labour, which raises a number of security issues for both states and people. Destination countries in the industrialized world focus almost exclusively on migration controls. The significance and length of the transit phase is often greatly under-estimated. Increasing restrictions in migration and asylum policy evidently do not stop or even diminish the flow of people, nor do they prevent their transit stay. Instead, restrictions have only managed to add to the human suffering without any real impact on migration flows. The European countries' apparent reliance on the current system is misplaced. The resilience and erratic nature of transit means that today's undocumented migrants in Greece or Morocco are tomorrow's irregular migrants or asylum seekers in the United Kingdom and Holland.

All the countries involved – from the EU's periphery, the EU's core to the EU's neighbours – will need to recognize that they are faced with a truly shared problem. Trying to pass the problem on has not brought any solution, either from the perspective of the migrants or from the perspective of the states. Migration flows are not one-off events that can be addressed with ad hoc measures. Transit migration is a process that is highly adaptable and contingent on a number of factors. What is more, transit migration is a state of insecurity that renders migrants and refugees particularly vulnerable. Addressing human suffering, safe-guarding fundamental rights, and delivering refugee protection at all stages of the migration cycle needs to become once again the priority. Recognizing the true dimension and impact of transit migration will be a necessary step in that direction.

Notes

1 Introduction

1 IOM defines transit in relation to air traffic as 'a stopover of passage, of varying length, while traveling between two or more countries, either incidental to continuous transportation, or for the purposes of changing planes or joining an ongoing flight or other mode of transport' (IOM, International Migration Law: Glossary on Migration, IOM, Geneva, 2004, p. 66), but this does not refer to the migration condition discussed in this book.
2 The same approach was also developed in Papadopoulou 2004, 2005a.
3 The Kurds were the biggest transit group in Greece at the time of my fieldwork in 2000–3. Today, the majority of transit migrants originate from Asia and Africa.
4 Fieldwork in Greece was conducted for the purpose of a PhD degree at Oxford University (2000–4) and funded by the Economic and Social Research Council (UK) and the Greek State Scholarships Foundation.
5 The names have been changed; even though this was partly unnecessary, as the Kurds had already invented 'protection' mechanisms by introducing themselves with different names to different people.

2 Migration in Europe

1 Communication from the Commission to the Council, the European Parliament, the Economic and Social Committee and the Committee of the Regions, Study on the links between legal and illegal migration, COM (2004) 412, 4.6.2004.
2 Green Paper on an EU approach to managing economic migration, COM (2004) 811, 11.1.2005; Communication from the Commission, Policy Plan on Legal Migration, COM (2005) 669 final, 21.12.2005.
3 Proposal for a comprehensive plan to combat illegal immigration and trafficking of human beings in the European Union, 2002/C 142/02, OJ 14.6.2002.
4 Council Directive 2002/90/EC of 28 November 2002 defining the facilitation of unauthorized entry, transit and residence, OJ 5.12.2002; Council Framework Decision of 28 November 2002 on the strengthening of the penal framework to prevent the facilitation of unauthorized entry, transit and residence (2002/946/JHA), OJ 5.12.2002.
5 Addressing mixed migratory movements: A 10-Point Plan of Action, UNHCR, June 2006.
6 Communication from the Commission on Policy Priorities in the fight against illegal migration of third-country nationals, COM (2006) 402 final, 19.7.2006; Communication from the Commission to the Council and the European Parliament, 'The global approach to migration one year on: towards a comprehensive European migration policy', COM (2006) 735 final, 30.11.2006.

  7 Proposal for a Directive of the European Parliament and of the Council providing for sanctions against employers of illegally staying third-country nationals, COM (2007) 249, 16.5.2007.
  8 Proposal for a Directive of the European Parliament and of the Council on common standards and procedures in member states for returning illegally staying third-country nationals, COM (2005) 391, 1.9.2005.
  9 Fortress Europe Blog: http://fortresseurope.blogspot.com
 10 The United Nations Convention on the Law of the Sea (UNCLOS, 1982); the International Convention for the Safety of Life at Sea (SOLAS, 1974); the International Convention on Maritime Search and Rescue (SAR, 1979); the Guidelines on the Treatment of Persons rescued at Sea, adopted by the Maritime Safety Committee Resolution 167 (May 2004); and, finally, the amendments to the SOLAS and SAR Conventions, adopted on 1 July 2006.
 11 Stated by the Representative of Malta at the European Parliament Public hearing on 'Tragedies of Migrants at Sea', Brussels, 3 July 2007.
 12 Commission Staff Working Document, 'Study on the international law instruments in relation to illegal migration by sea', SEC (2007) 691, 15.5.2007.
 13 Council Directive 2003/9/EC of 27 January 2003 laying down minimum standards for the reception of asylum seekers, OJ 6.2.2003; Council Directive 2005/85/EC of 1 December 2005 on minimum standards on procedures in member states for granting and withdrawing refugee status, OJ 13.12.2005; Council Directive 2004/83/EC of 29 April 2004 on minimum standards for the qualification and status of third-country nationals or stateless persons as refugees or as persons who otherwise need international protection and the content of the protection granted, OJ 30.9.2004; Council Regulation No 343/2003 of 18 February 2003 establishing the criteria and mechanisms for determining the member state responsible for examining an asylum application lodged in one of the member states by a third-country national, OJ 25.2.2003.
 14 European Commission (2007), 'Non-transposition of 2 Directives in the field of immigration and asylum: Commission delivers reasoned opinions', Press Release 7 July 2007.
 15 Green Paper on the future Common European Asylum System, COM (2007) 301, 6.6.2007.
 16 Finnish Presidency (2006), 'Migration Management; Extended European Solidarity in Immigration, Border Control and Asylum Policies', Document for the Informal JHA Ministerial Meeting Tampere, 20–22 September 2006.
 17 German Presidency Draft Council Resolution on burden-sharing, Council Document 7773/94 ASIM 124, July 1994.
 18 Report from the Commission to the European Parliament and the Council on the evaluation of the Dublin system, COM (2007) 299, 6.6.2007.
 19 Council Note from Presidency to Coreper, 'A strategy for the external dimension of JHA: Global freedom, security and justice', 14366/05, 11 November 2005.
 20 Communication from the Commission to the Council and the European Parliament, Priority actions for responding to the challenges of migration, First follow-up to the Hampton Court, COM (2005) 621, 30.11.2005.

21 Communication from the Commission to the Council, the European Parliament, the Economic and Social Committee and the Committee of the Regions, Migration and Development: some concrete orientations, COM (2005) 390, 1.9.2005.
22 Communication from the Commission to the Council, the European Parliament, the Economic and Social Committee and the Committee of the Regions, On circular migration and mobility partnerships between the European Union and third countries, COM(2007) 248, 16.5.2007.
23 A feasibility study and project description are underway, see 'Answer given by Mr Michel on behalf of the Commission (30.8.2007)', E-2680/07EN, on Written question by Robert Kilroy-Silk: http://www.europarl.europa.eu/sides/getAllAnswers.do?reference=E-2007-2680&language=SL
24 Communication from the Commission to the Council, the European Parliament, the Economic and Social Committee and the Committee of the Regions, Applying the Global Approach to Migration to the Eastern and South-Eastern Regions Neighbouring the European Union, COM(2007) 247, 16.5.2007.
25 European Commission, Strategy Paper for the Thematic Programme of Cooperation with Third Countries in the Areas of Migration and Asylum, Multiannual indicative programme 2007–2010.
26 Ibid.
27 Communication from the Commission to the Council and the European Parliament on Regional Protection Programmes, COM (2005) 388, 1.9.2005.
28 European Commission EuropeAid Cooperation Office, List of projects from the Call for Proposals 2004 and 2005: http://ec.europa.eu/europeaid/where/worldwide/migrationasylum/documents/projets_aeneas_2004_2005.pdf
29 The author witnessed and had first-hand experience of the content, aims, objectives and outcomes of this particular EC-funded project with UNHCR, having held the post of Coordinator of the project in the year 2005. The views expressed in this book are strictly those of the author and do not represent the views of UNHCR.

3   Transit in Europe: The Case of Greece

1 The peak in applications for that year can be largely ascribed to the mass arrival of Iraqi refugees, for whom Greece was the first European country they could reach, even on foot. It is also a result of the application by the Greek authorities of special procedures introduced to clear the backlog of asylum seekers (UNHCR, 2007a). These qualifications do not, however, minimize the overall importance of migration and asylum numbers in Greece, which is also confirmed over a longer period of time.
2 'Metron Analysis' survey conducted for the Ministry of Interior on a sample of 2000 migrants, published in *Eleftherotypia* newspaper, 1 August 2001.
3 See, for example, Labrianidis L. and Lyberaki A. (2001), Triantafyllidou and Gropas (2006).
4 *Asylum Levels and Trends: Europe and Non-European Industrialized Countries*, 2003, UNHCR Population and Data Unit, UNHCR, 24 February 2004, p. 5 and Table 2.

5　UNHCR, 2006, *Global Trends*, Revision 16 July 2007, Table 7.
6　Mentioned by the Minister of Public Order to the European Parliament LIBE Committee delegation to Greece in June 2007, see European Parliament (2007).
7　*Agence Europe Presse*, 8 October 2007.
8　*Athens News* newspaper, 22 June 2007.
9　*Ta Nea* newspaper, 7 May 2007.
10　The European Sea Border Control Centre is also located in Piraeus, Greece.
11　Turkey has signed readmission agreements with Syria, Kyrgyzstan and Romania, and is currently negotiating agreements with many source countries in the former Soviet Union, Middle East and Asia.
12　Interview with Greek Ministry of Foreign Affairs, Turkey Desk, 8 April 2003.
13　*Agence Europe Press*, 8 October 2007.
14　See MIREM (Return Migration to the Maghreb) database on readmission agreements in the website: http://www.mirem.eu/docs/rapports-ed-documents/grece
15　The UK data refers to decision taken on applications at first instance; administrative review decisions had a recognition rate of 24.4 per cent in 2006, UNHCR, 2006, *Global Trends*, Revision 16 July 2007, Table 7.
16　*Final Evaluation of the European Refugee Fund for the Period 2000–4*, (2006), Commission Staff Working Document, p. 5.
17　New Democracy MP Karatasos, Parliamentary Proceedings, Session 4 April 1997, p. 5414.
18　Interview with NGO 'Voluntary Work Athens', 16 October 2001, and Médecins du Monde Press release 20 January 1997.
19　'The Strike Committee', Press release, 7 November 1996, and *Eleftherotypia*, 9 November 1996.
20　'Bi-partisan Committee for Foreigners and Minority Issues', Athens Local Council, Press release, 18 November 1996, and UNHCR Athens, Press Release, 21 February 1997.
21　*Athens News*, 4 November 1996.
22　Ministry of Health, Press release, 20 December 1996, and Committee of the Refugees of Aghios Andreas, Press release, 8 February 1997.
23　Medecins sans Frontieres, Refugee Camp of Aghios Andreas Situation Report 3, 23 December 1996, also *Eleftherotypia*, 21 December 1996 and 6 June 1997.
24　Greek Committee for International Democratic Solidarity, Resolution, 4 February 1998, signed by the main trade unions: General Confederation of Greek Workers, General Confederation of Civil Servants, Athens Labour Centre, Federation of Women of Greece, Athens Bar Association, etc.
25　Newspapers: *Eleftherotypia*, 15 February 1997; *Avgi*, 7 February 1997 and 19 February 1997; and *Kathimerini*, 22 May 1997.
26　*Avgi* newspaper, 25 February 1997.
27　Mentioned in Parliamentary Proceedings, Session 12 January 1998, pp. 4090–2
28　Internationale Föderation Iranischer Flüchtlinge – Immigranten RäteVerband Deutschland, fax 16 October 1997.
29　*Athens News*, 20 May 1997, and Médecins du Monde, (1998).
30　President of the Refugee Committee, Press conference organized by the 'Network in Support of Migrants and Refugees' (Diktyo), 22 May 1998.

31 Letter by the President of the Committee of Iraqi Refugees to Amnesty International, 15 November 1998.
32 Interview with NGO 'Voluntary Work Athens', 16 October 2001.
33 *Ta Nea*, 16 February 1999, 17 February 1999, 24 February 1999.
34 Ibid., 17 February 1999.
35 Ibid., 18 February 1999.
36 Ibid., 17 February 1999.
37 Greek-Kurdish Solidarity Committee, 'Support the Kurdish refugees', leaflet, 21 June 2000; Anti-War Initiative of Nea Smyrni, Leaflet.
38 Interview with member of the Committee, 9 July 2002, Interview with social worker in the Nea Smyrni Council, 18 July 2002.
39 Newspapers, *Eleftherotypia*, 16 May 2001; *Exousia*, 5 July 1997; *Peloponissos Patron*, 7 August 1997.
40 'The groups of Kurdish refugees in Loutraki camp', letter 20 February 1998; *Ta Nea*, 12 January 1998; *Eleftherotypia*, 15 January 2002 and 16 January 2002.
41 Vimagazino, supplement to newspaper, *To Vima*, 26 August 2007.
42 BBC News, 18 September 2007.
43 Vice Minister of Health and Welfare Farmakis, Parliamentary Proceedings, Session 5 February 1999, p. 4098.
44 Vice-Minister of Health Kotsonis, Parliamentary Proceedings, Session 22 October 1998, p. 820.

4   Being in Transit

1 M. Jandl, *Estimates on the numbers of illegal and smuggled immigrants in Europe*, International Centre for Migration Policy Development (ICMPD), Eighth International Metropolis Conference, 17 September 2003.
2 According to the UN Convention against Transnational Organized Crime, smuggling is defined as: 'The procurement in order to obtain directly or indirectly a financial or other material benefit of the illegal entry of person into a state party of which the person is not a national or permanent resident' [Article 3, Smuggling Protocol].
3 See also Salt and Stein (1997), İçduygu and Toktas (2002), Papadopoulou (2004), Iselin and Adams (2003), van Liempt (2007).
4 D. Serge, *Gao, couloir de transit pour l'Europe, 'Carnets de route'*, Radio France International (RFI), 17 October 2005.
5 Articles 6,3(b); 9,1(a); 14,2(e); 16,1; 16,2; 16,3; 16,4; 19,1; 19,2.
6 International Convention Relating to Stowaways, International Maritime Organization, 1957. The Convention is not ratified so as to enter into international law, but still remains the standard definition.
7 Morrison and Crosland (2001) have argued that the refusal to disembark asylum-seeker stowaways at European destinations might also breach the standards set in the Safety Of Lives At Sea (SOLAS) Convention.
8 *Kathimerini*, 28 September 2007.
9 Ibid., 29 August 2002.
10 Cited in *Agence Europe Press*, 8 October 2007.
11 *Ta Nea*, 5 January 1998.

12　Fortress Europe Blog information on deaths of migrants at borders collected by country – data up to 30 September 2007: http://fortresseurope.blogspot. com/2006/01/i-numeri-dellegeo-anno-per-anno.html

13　*Ta Nea*, 3 November 1999.

14　*Eleftherotypia*, 8 January 2001, 26 January 2001, 26 May 2001.

15　*Athens News*, 11 August 1998.

16　See also van Liempt and Doomernik (2006).

17　'Report-proposal for the solution to the problems of homeless refugees-Kurds in the municipality of Nea Smyrni', Nea Smyrni Municipality, Social Policy Office, 2002, (in Greek).

18　The state of permanent tension that refugees experience during this transitional phase has also been described as 'liminality' (Harrel-Bond and Voutira, 1992, Kaytaz, 2006).

19　The Kurdish political organizations active in Greece throughout the 1990s have been: from Turkey, PKK (through its political wing ERNK), Kurdish Red Crescent and Kurdish Cultural Centre, PRK-Rizgari (Liberation Party of Kurdistan), DHKP-C (Revolutionary People's Liberation Front), and the related Turkish TIKKO/TKP-ML (Workers' and Peasants' Liberation Army of Turkey/Turkish Communist Party) and the PSK (Kurdistan Socialist Party); from Iraq, KDP (Kurdistan Democratic Party), and PUK (Patriotic Union of Kurdistan); from Iran PDKI (Democratic Party of Iranian Kurdistan) and Komala; and from Syria, YEKITI (Kurdish Democratic Union of Syria in Greece) and the KDP-Syria (Kurdistan Democratic Party-Syria).

20　The Voice of Kurdistan, *ERNK Magazine*, 75, March–June 2001 (in Greek).

5　Transit in the Maghreb: Sub-Saharans and *el-harga*

1　Fortress Europe blog, 2006.

2　BBC, Monday 2 July 2007.

3　Ibid.

4　*Le Monde* newspaper, 11 July 2003.

5　European Commission (2004), ENP Country Report, Tunisia, Commission Staff Working paper, COM(2004)373, 12.5.2004.

6　*Nouvel Observateur* magazine, 5 October 2004.

7　European Commission (2004), ENP Country Report, Tunisia, Commission Staff Working paper, COM(2004)373, 12.5.2004.

8　*El Watan* newspaper, 18 June 2007.

9　Information about the authorization granted to the ICRC in: 'Commentaires à propos de la communication de la Commission Européenne intitulée "Communication de la Commission Européenne au Conseil et au Parlement Européens": Rapport de suivi –Politique Européenne de Voisinage-Tunisie: http://www.tunisieinfo.com/tunisie-eu.html

10　See MIREM (Return Migration the Maghreb), EUI/ RSCAS, *Inventory of the agreements linked to readmission,* on the website: http://www.mirem.eu/ datasets/agreements/reports-and-documents

11　*Liberation* newspaper, 6 July 2006.

12　Middle East Online, 6 March 2007.

13　Ibid.

14   *Agence France Presse*, 22 February 2007.
15   European Council for Refugees and Exiles, *ECRAN Weekly*, 19 March 2007.
16   European Commission (2004), Report of the Technical Mission to Libya on Illegal Immigration 27 November – 06 December 2004.
17   European Parliament mission to Libya, Press Release, 7 December 2005.
18   MPI Global Data Center, Italy: Stock of foreign population by country of nationality, 1985 to 2003: http://www.migrationinformation.org/
19   *Maroc Hebdo International* magazine, No. 577, 24–30 October 2003.
20   *Le Quotidien d'Oran* newspaper, 14 October 2003.
21   *L'Expression* newspaper, 9 June 2007.
22   Ibid.
23   *Maroc Hebdo International*, No. 699, 14–20 October 2005.
24   *TelQuel* magazine, No. 274, 25 May 2007.
25   *Jeune Afrique* magazine, 18 November 2002.
26   *Maroc Hebdo International*, No. 699, 14–20 October 2005.
27   ANSA English Media Service, 11 November 2003.
28   A residence card will be issued also to a *'foreign national who has obtained refugee status under the provisions of the ordinance of 29th of August 1957 applying the [1951] Convention … as well as his/her spouse and their minor children'* (Article 17, para. 5).
29   UNHCR Global Refugee Trends 2005 and UNHCR Global Refugee Trends 2003.
30   The total number of casualties is uncertain, as Morocco and Spain give contradictory information.
31   See, for example, the article in the daily *Aujourd'hui*, 'Le Maroc passe a l'étranger pour un pays qui maltraite et tue des clandestins subsahariens', *Aujourd'hui Le Maroc* newspaper, 10 October 2005.
32   'Open letter by Moroccan, African and European associations', published on the site of Migreurop, 4 January 2007: http://www.migreurop.org/article1035.html
33   Indicatively: CESAM (Conseil des migrants subsahariens au Maroc), RSF-Maroc (Rassemblement des réfugiés ivoiriens au Maroc, Réfugiés sans frontières-Maroc), AIPDRDA (Association Interafricaine pour la promotion et la défense des droits des réfugiés et demandeurs d'asile), Ligue des familles africaines, ASDHOM (Association de défense des droits de l'homme au Maroc), Pateras de Vida, GADEM (Groupe anti-raciste d'accompagnement et de défense des étrangers et migrants), AFVIC (Amis et familles des victimes de l'immigration clandestine).
34   *TelQuel* magazine, May 2007.
35   The OAU Convention governing the specific aspects of refugee problems in Africa (1969) also defines a refugee as a person who is a victim of generalized violence and aggression, which is not included in the 1951 Geneva Convention, see Article1 (2): *'the term "refugee" shall also apply to every person who, owing to external aggression, occupation, foreign domination or events seriously disturbing public order in either part or the whole of his country of origin or nationality, is compelled to leave his place of habitual residence in order to seek refuge in another place outside his country of origin or nationality.'*

6 Transit in the East: Shifting Borders

1 Eurostat, *Population statistics: Detailed tables*, Luxembourg; 2006 edition; and Eurostat, 'Population and Social Conditions: Migration and asylum', data 1995–2006.
2 UNHCR, *Global refugee trends* 2003, 2004, 2005 and 2006.
3 BBC, 11 May 2005.
4 UNHCR, Country Operations Plan, Czech Republic, 2006.
5 BBC, 10 August 2000.
6 Ibid., 2 November 2001.
7 Ibid., 19 August 2002.
8 Ibid., 14 February 2003.
9 Ibid., 1 April 2007.
10 UNHCR, *Regional Operations Plan, Western Newly Independent States: Belarus, Moldova and Ukraine*, Overview, 2006.
11 BBC, 13 December 2002.
12 UNHCR, Country Operations Plan, Russia, 2006.
13 BBC, 17 October 2006.
14 Ibid., 23 February 2004.

Bibliography

Alioua, M. (2005), Sub-Saharan cross-national migration to North African countries: The Moroccan stage, *Maghreb-Machrek*, 185, 37–57.

Aliyev, A. (2006), Migration to and from Azerbaijan, in: Rios, R. (ed.), *Planning and Managing Labour Migration*, Migration Perspectives Eastern Europe and Central Asia, IOM, October.

Alscher, S. (2005), *Knocking at the Doors of 'Fortress Europe': Migration and Border Control in Southern Spain and Eastern Poland*, CCIS Working Paper 126, University of California, San Diego.

André, M. and Charlet, F. (2007), Investing for the future: Capacity building in Morocco, *Forced Migration Review*, 28, July.

Andreas, P. (2001), The transformation of migrant smuggling across the US-Mexican border, in: Kyle, D. and Koslowski, R. (eds), *Global Human Smuggling: Comparative Perspectives*, Baltimore, MD: The Johns Hopkins University Press.

Andrijasevic, R. (2006), *How to Balance Rights and Responsibilities on Asylum at the EU's Southern Borders of Italy and Libya*, CPS, Central European University, 2005/6

Antonopoulos, G. and Winterdyk, J., The smuggling of migrants in Greece: An examination of its social organization, *European Journal of Criminology*, 3(4), 439–61.

APDH (Asociación Pro-Derechos Humanos de Andalucía) (2007), *Derechos Humanos en la Frontera Sur 2006*, January.

Arango, J. and Jachimowizc, M. (2005), *Regularizing Immigrants in Spain: A New Approach*, Migration Information Source, Feature Story, MPI, Washington.

Ba, O. C. and Choplin, A. (2005), Tenter l'Aventure par la Mauritanie: Migrations transsahariennes et recompositions urbaines, *Autrepart*, 36, 21–42.

Baba, N. (2006), *Mineurs marocains non accompagnes. Quelle réalité pour le retour?*, MIREM Project, Migration de Retour au Maghreb, Florence; European University Institute/Robert Schuman Centre for Advanced Studies.

Bade, K. (2003), *Legal and Illegal Immigration into Europe: Experiences and Challenges*, Netherlands Institute for Advanced Study (NIAS).

Bailey, A., Wright, R., Mountz, A. and Miyares, I. (2002) (Re)producing Salvadoran transnational geographies, *Annals of the Association of American Geographers*, 92(1), 125–44.

Barjaba, K. (2004), *Albania: Looking Beyond Borders*, Migration Information Source, Country Profile, Migration Information Source, MPI, Washington

Bensaad, A. (2003), Agadez, Carrefour migratoire sahelo-maghrebin, *Revue Européenne des Migrations Internationales*, 19.

Bilger, V., Hofman, M. and Jandl, M. (2006), Human smuggling as a transnational service industry: Evidence from Austria, *International Migration*, 44(4), 59–93.

Black, R. (1992), *Livelihood and Vulnerability of Foreign Refugees in Greece*, Department of Geography, Kings College, London, Occasional Paper, 33.

Black, R. (1994), Political refugees or economic migrants? Kurdish and Assyrian refugees in Greece, *Migration: A European Journal of International Migration and Ethnic Relations*, 1994–1995, 25, 79–109

Boswell, C. (2003), Burden-sharing in the European Union: Lessons from the UK and Germany, *Journal of Refugee Studies*, 16 (3), 317–35.

Boubakri, H. (2004), *Transit Migration between Tunisia, Libya and Sub-Saharan Africa: Study Based on Greater Tunis*, Council of Europe Regional Conference, on 'Migrants in transit countries: Sharing responsibility for management and protection', Istanbul 30 September – 1 October 2004.

Boubakri, H. and Mazella, S. (2005), La Tunisie entre transit et immigration: Politiques migratoires et conditions d'accueil des migrants africains à Tunis, *Autrepart*, 36, IRD, 149–65.

Boyd, M. (1989), Family and personal networks in international migration: Recent developments and new agendas, *International Migration Review*, 23 (3), 638–62.

Brechat, J. (2005), Migrants, Transporteurs et Agents d'Etat. Recontre sur l'axe Agadez-Sebha, *Autrepart*, 36, 43–62.

Bredeloup, S. and Pliez, O. (2006), Migrations entre les deux rives du Sahara, *Autrepart: Revue de sciences sociales au Sud*, 36, IRD.

Brewer, K. and Yükseker, D. (2006), *A Survey on African Migrants and Asylum Seekers in Istanbul*, MiReKoc Research Projects 2005–2006.

Buldekbaev, M. (2006), Every migrant has the right to [Il]legal employment?, in: Rios, R.(ed.), *Planning and Managing Labour Migration*, Migration Perspectives Eastern Europe and Central Asia, IOM, October.

Carling, J. (2007a), Migration Control and Migrant Fatalities at the Spanish-African Borders, *International Migration Review*, 41(2), 316–43.

Carling, J. (2007b), *The Merits and Limitations of Spain's High-Tech Border Control*, Migration Information Source, Migration Information Source, MPI, Washington.

Carrera, S. and Guild, E. (2007), *An EU Framework on Sanctions against Employers of Irregular Immigrants: Some Reflections on the Scope, Features & Added Value*, CEPS Policy Brief, No. 140, August.

Cassarino, J.-P. and Fargues, P. (2006), Policy Responses in MENA Countries of Transit for Migrants: An Analytical Framework for Policy-Making, in: Sorensen, N. (ed.), *Mediterranean Transit Migration*, Copenhagen: Danish Institute for International Studies.

Castles, S. (2006), *Back to the Future? Can Europe meet its Labour Needs through Temporary Migration?*, International Migration Institute, James Martin 21st Century School, University of Oxford, Working Paper No. 1.

Cavounidis, J. (2002), Migration in Southern Europe and the Case of Greece, *International Migration*, 40(1), 45–70.

Cavounidis, J. and Hatzaki, L. (1999), *Foreigners Applying for Temporary Residence Card: Citizenship, Gender and Area of Settlement*, Athens, National Labour Institute, 1999.

Charef, M. (2004), *La situation géographique comme facteur facilitant la migration irrégulière dans un pays de transit: Cas de Tanger (Maroc)*, Council of Europe Regional Conference, on 'Migrants in transit countries: Sharing responsibility for management and protection', Istanbul 30 September – 1 October 2004.

Chatelard, G. (2002), *Iraqi Forced Migrants in Jordan: Conditions, Religious Networks and the Smuggling Process*, Robert Schuman Centre for Advanced Studies, Working Paper, No. 50, European University Institute, Florence.

CIMADE (2004), *La Situation Alarmante des Migrants SubSahariens en transit au Maroc et les Conséquences des politiques de l'Union Européenne*, CIMADE: Paris.

Collyer, M. (2004), *Undocumented sub-Saharan African Migrants in Morocco*, Paper presented to the dialogue on Mediterranean Transit Migration Conference organized by DIIS and ICMPD, Copenhagen.

Collyer, M. (2006), *States of Insecurity: Consequences of Saharan Transit Migration*, Centre on Migration Policy and Society, University of Oxford, Working Paper No. 31.

Council of Europe (CoE) (2004), Regional Conference on migration, 'Migrants in the transit countries: sharing responsibilities in management and protection', Proceedings, Istanbul 30 September – 1 October 2004.

Council of Europe (CoE), 2007, *Regularisation Programmes for Irregular Migrants*, Parliamentary Assembly, Committee on Migration, Refugees and Population, 11 September 2007.

Crisp, J. (1999), *Policy Challenges and New Diasporas: Migrant Networks and their Impacts on Asylum Flows and Regimes*, Transnational Communities Working Papers, WPTC-99-05, online paper available at:
http://www.transcomm.ox.ac.uk

Danis, D. (2006), *Integration in Limbo, Iraqi, Afghan and Maghrebi Migrants in Istanbul*, MiReKoc Research Programmes 2005–2006, Istanbul.

De Haas, H. (2005), *Morocco: From Emigration Country to Africa's Migration Passage to Europe*, Migration Information Source Country Profile, MPI, Washington.

De Haas, H. (2007), Morocco's migration experience: A transitional perspective, *International Migration*, 45(4), 39–70.

Drbohlav, D. (2005), *The Czech Republic: From Liberal Policy to EU Membership*, Migration Information Source, Country Profile, MPI, Washington.

Düvell, F. (2006*) Crossing the Fringes of Europe: Transit Migration in the EU's Neighbourhood*, Centre on Migration, Policy and Society, Working Paper No. 33, University of Oxford.

ECRE (2006), *Europe's Asylum Rules Put Lives at Risk and Cause Suffering*, New Release, 26 June, Brussels: ECRE.

ECRE (2007), *The Dublin Regulation: Twenty Voices – Twenty Reasons for Change*, Brussels: ECRE.

European Economic and Social Committee (EESC) (2002), Plenary session, Summary of Opinions adopted, Brussels 13 December 2002, EESC Registry 232/2002 FR-EN-IT-ES/RK/NT/nm.

European Parliament (2005), *Report from the LIBE Committee Delegation on the Visit to the Temporary Holding Centre (THC) in Lampedusa*, 19 September.

European Parliament (2006a), *Trends in the Different Legislations of the Member States Concerning Asylum in the EU: The Human Cost of Border Control*, Briefing Paper, Directorate General Internal Policies, IPOL/C/LIBE/FWC/2005-23-SCI PE 378.258.

European Parliament (2006b), *Report from the LIBE Committee Delegation on the Visit to Ceuta and Melilla*, 24 January.

European Parliament (2006c), *Report by the LIBE Committee Delegation on Its Visit to the Administrative Detention Centres in Malta*, 30 March.

European Parliament (2006d), *Report from the LIBE Committee Delegation on the Visit to Tenerife and Fuerteventura*, 6 July.

European Parliament (2007), *Report from the LIBE Committee Delegation on the Visit to Greece (Samos and Athens)*, 2 July.

Faist T. (2000), *The Volumes and Dynamics of International Migration and Transnational Social Spaces*, Oxford: Oxford University Press.

Fakiolas, R. (1999), Greece, in: Angenendt, S. (ed.), *Asylum and Migration Policies in the European Union*, Research Institute of the German Society for Foreign Affairs, Bonn: Union Europa Verlag.

Fickenauer, J. (2001), Russian transnational organised crime and human trafficking, in: Kyle, D. and Koslowski, R. (eds), *Global Human Smuggling: Comparative Perspectives*, Baltimore, MD: The John Hopkins University Press.

Frantz, E. (2003), *Report on the Situation of Refugees in Turkey: Findings of a Five-Week Exploratory Study, December 2002 – January 2003*, American University in Cairo (AUC).

Frattini, F. (2007), 'Shaping Migration Patterns,' Speech in the European Parliament, 20 September.

Futo, P., Jandl, M. and Karsakova, L. (2005), Illegal migration and human smuggling in Central and Eastern Europe, *Migracijske i etničke teme* 21(1–2), 35–54.

Geddes, A., 2005, Europeanization goes south: The external dimension of EU migration and asylum policy, *Zeitschrift für Staats- und Europawissenschaften*, 3(2), 275–93.

Giacca, G. (2004), *Clandestini ou le problème de la politique migratoire en Italie*, UNHCR New Issues in Refugee Research, Working Paper No. 101.

Gil-Bazo, M. (2006), *Refugee Status, Subsidiary Protection, and the Right to be Granted Asylum under EC Law*, UNHCR New Issues in Refugee Research, Working Paper No. 33.

Goldschmidt, E. (2006), Storming the fences: Morocco and Europe's Anti-Migration Policy, *Middle East Report*, 239, Summer.

Gorny, A. and Ruspini, P. (2004), *Migration in the New Europe: East and West Revisited*, Basingstoke: Palgrave Macmillan.

Griffiths, D. (2002), *Somali and Kurdish Refugees in London: New Identities in the Diaspora*, Aldershot: Ashgate.

Hammersley, M. (1992), *What's Wrong with Ethnography? Methodological Explorations*, London: Routledge.

Hammouda, N. E. (2005), Algérie: démographie et économie des migrations, in: Fargues, P. (ed.), *Mediterranean Migration – 2005 Report*, pp. 64–74, Florence: European University Institute/Robert Schuman Centre for Advanced Studies, CARIM.

Hamood, S. (2006), *African Transit Migration Through Libya to Europe: The Human Cost*, American University in Cairo (AUC)

Harrel-Bond, B. and Voutira, E. (1992), Anthropology and the study of refugees, *Anthropology Today*, 8(4), 6–10.

Hatziprokopiou, P. (2003), Albanian immigrants in Thessaloniki, Greece: Processes of economic and social incorporation, *Journal of Ethnic and Migration Studies*, 29(6), 1033–57.

Heleniak, T. (2002), *Migration Dilemmas Haunt Post-Soviet Russia*, Migration Information Source, Country Profiles, MPI, Washington.

Hirschon, R. (1998), *Heirs of the Greek Catastrophe: The Social Life of Asia Minor Refugees in Piraeus*, New York; Oxford: Berghahn Books.

Home Office (2006), *Country of Origin Information Report*, Algeria, April 2006.

Human Rights Watch (2006), *Libya – Stemming the Flow: Abuses against Migrants, Asylum Seekers and Refugees*, Part III, 18(5), September 2006.

İçduygu, A. (1995), Transit Migrants and Turkey, *Bogazici Journal: Review of Social, Economic and Administrative Studies*, 10(1–2), 127–42.

İçduygu, A. (2000), The Politics of International Migratory Regimes: Transit Migration Flows in Turkey, *International Journal of Social Sciences*, 165, 357–67.

İçduygu, A. (2003), *Irregular Migration in Turkey*, IOM.

İçduygu, A. (2005), *Transit Migration in Turkey: Trends, Patterns and Issues*, CARIM report, Florence: European University Institute/Robert Schuman Centre for Advanced Studies

İçduygu, A. (2004), Transborder Crime between Greece and Turkey: Human Smuggling and its Regional Consequences, *Southeast European and Black Sea Studies*, 4(2), 294–314.

İçduygu, A. and Toktas, S. (2002), How do smuggling and trafficking operate via irregular border-crossings in the Middle East? Evidence from fieldwork in Turkey, *International Migration*, 40(6), 25–54.

ICMPD (2005), *Overview of the Migration Systems in the CIS Countries*, Vienna, September.

Iglicka, K. (2005), *EU Membership Highlights Poland's Migration Challenges*, Migration Information Source, Country Profiles, MPI, Washington.

Iglicka, K. and Weinar, A. (2006), *Immigration to Poland: The Case of Ukrainians*, report prepared for the Research Project MIGSYS, 'Immigrants, policies and migration systems: An ethnographic comparative approach, Eliamep, July.

International Maritime Organization (IMO) (2007), *Reports on Stowaway Incidents*, May to July 2007, London: IMO.

IOM (1996), *Transit Migration in Turkey*, Migration Information Programme, Budapest.

IOM (1994), *Transit Migration in Ukraine*, Migration Information Programme, IOM, August.

IOM (1994), *Transit Migration in the Russian Federation*, Migration Information Programme, IOM, July.

IOM (1994), *Transit Migration in Poland*, Migration Information Programme, IOM, April.

IOM (1994), *Transit Migration in Hungary*, Migration Information Programme, IOM, December.

IOM (2003), *Study on Transit Migration through Azerbaijan*, IOM: Azerbaijan.

IOM (2004), *International Migration Law: Glossary on Migration*, IOM: Geneva.

IOM (2006), *Baseline Research on Smuggling of Migrants in, from and through Central Asia*, IOM Technical Cooperation Centre for Europe and Central Asia, Vienna.

Iselin, B. and Adams, M. (2003), *Distinguishing between Human Trafficking and People Smuggling*, UN Office on Drugs and Crime (UNDOC), Regional Centre for East Asia and the Pacific.

Ivakhniouk, I. (2004), *Analysis of Economic, Social, Demographic and Political Basis of Transit Migration in Russia – Moscow Case*, paper presented at the Council of Europe Regional Conference on 'Migrants in transit countries: Sharing responsibility for management and protection', Istanbul 30 September–1 October 2004.

Ivakhniouk, I. (2006), *Migration in the CIS Region: Common Problems and Mutual Benefits*, International symposium on international migration and development, Population Division, Department of Economic and Social Affairs, United Nations Secretariat, 28 June 2006.

Jandl, M. (2003), *Moldova Seeks Stability Amid Mass Emigration*, Migration Information Source, Country Paper, MPI, Washington.

Juhasz, J. (1999), *Illegal Labour Migration and Employment in Hungary*, International Migration Papers, ILO: Geneva.

Juhasz, J. (2003), *Hungary: Transit Country Between East and West*, Migration Information Source, Country Paper, MPI, Washington.

Kasimis, C. and Kassimi, C. (2004), *Greece: A History of Migration*, Migration Information Source, MPI, Washington.

Kaytaz, E. (2006), *Turkey as a Country of Transit Migration: The Case of Christian Iranian Asylum Seekers*, MPhil Thesis, University of Oxford.

Kirişçi, K. (2003), *Turkey: A Transformation from Emigration to Immigration*, Migration Information Source, Country Paper, MPI, Washington.

Kneebone, S. (2005), *The Legal and Ethical Implications of Extra-Territorial Processing of Asylum Seekers: The Safe Third Country Concept*, article based on a paper presented to the 'Moving On: Forced Migration and Human Rights Conference', Sydney 22 November 2005.

Korac, M. (2001), *Dilemmas of Integration: Two Policy Contexts and Refugee Strategies for Integration*, A comparative study of the integration experiences of refugees from Former Yugoslavia in Rome and Amsterdam, Final report, Refugee Studies Centre, Oxford University.

Koser, K. (1997), Social networks and the asylum cycle: The case of Iranians in the Netherlands, *International Migration Review*, 31(3), 591–611.

Koser, K. (2001), New approaches to asylum? *International Migration*, 39(6), 85–101.

Koser, K. and Gilbert, A. (2006), Coming to the UK: What do Asylum-Seekers Know About the UK before Arrival?, *Journal of Ethnic and Migration Studies*, 32(7), 1209–25

Kyle, D. and Dale, J. (2001), Smuggling the state back in: Agents of human smuggling reconsidered, in: Kyle, D., and Koslowski, R. (eds), *Global Human Smuggling: Comparative Perspectives,* Baltimore, MD: The Johns Hopkins University Press.

Kyle, D., and Koslowski, R. (eds) (2001), *Global Human Smuggling: Comparative Perspectives*, Baltimore, MD: The Johns Hopkins University Press.

Labrianidis, L. and Lyberaki, A. (2001), *Albanian Migrants in Thessaloniki: Paths of Prosperity and Oversights of Their Public Image*, Thessaloniki: Paratiritis (in Greek).

Landmine Monitor, Greece Report (2006), online report available at: http://www.icbl.org/lm/2006/greece.html

Lauth-Baccas, U. (2006), *The Sea Route to Europe: Migrant Illegal Entries to Lesvos Without Documents*, paper presented at the IMEPO Conference 'Migration in Greece: Experiences–Policies –Perspectives', Athens Greece, 23–24 November 2006.

Lavenex, S. (1999), *Safe Third Countries: Extending the EU Asylum and Immigration Policies to Central and Eastern Europe*, Budapest: CEU Press.

Lindstrom, C. (2005), European Union Policy on Asylum and Immigration. Addressing the Root Causes of Forced Migration: A Justice and Home Affairs

Policy of Freedom, Security and Justice?, *Social Policy & Administration*, 39(6), 587–605.

Malynovska, O. (2004), *International Migration in Contemporary Ukraine: Trends and Policy*, Global Commission on International Migration (GCIM), Global Migration Perspectives, No. 14, October.

Malynovska, O. (2006), *Caught Between East and West, Ukraine Struggles with Its Migration Policy*, Migration Information Source, Country Paper, MPI, Washington.

Massey, D., Alarcon, R., Durand, J. and Gonzalez, H. (1987), *Return to Aztlan: The Social Process of International Migration from Western Mexico*, Berkeley: University of California Press.

Mavris, L. (2002), Human smuggling and social networks: Transit migration through the states of Former Yugoslavia, *UNHCR, New Issues in Refugee Research*, Working Paper No. 72.

Médecins du Monde (1998), *Programme for Sheltering Displaced Asylum Seekers in a Camp in Penteli-Athens*, MdM Greek Delegation.

Mellah, F. (2000), *Clandestin en Méditerranée*, Paris; le cherche midi éditeur.

Migreurop (2006), *Guerre aux migrants: le livre noir sur Ceuta et Melilla*, June.

Morrison, J. and Crosland, B. (2001), The smuggling and trafficking of Refugees: The end game in European asylum policy? UNHCR, *New Issues in Refugee Research*, Working Paper No. 39.

Noll, G. (2000), *Negotiating Asylum*, The Hague: Nijhoff.

Noll, G. (2003), Risky games? A theoretical approach to burden-sharing in the asylum field, *Journal of Refugee Studies*, 16(3), 236–52.

O'Brien, L. (2003), *The Experience of Asylum Seekers Entering Greece*, Masters Thesis (MA) in Refugee Studies, University of East London.

Ortega-Perez, N. (2003), *Spain: Forging an Immigration Policy, Migration Information Source*, Country Profiles, MPI, Washington.

Ostergaard-Nielsen, E. (2000), *Turkish and Kurdish Transnational Political Mobilization in Germany and the Netherlands*, Transnational Communities Working Paper, WPTC-01-22, available at:
http://www.transcomm.ox.ac.uk

Papadimitriou, P. N. and Papageorgiou, I. F. (2005), The new 'Dubliners': An appraisal of Council Regulation 343/2003 (Dublin II) by the Greek authorities one year after its entry into force, *Journal of Refugee Studies*, 18(3), 299–318.

Papadopoulou, A. (2004), Smuggling into Europe: Transit migrants in Greece, *Journal of Refugee Studies*, 17(2), 169–86.

Papadopoulou, A. (2005a), Exploring the asylum-migration nexus: A case of transit migrants in Europe, Global Commission on International Migration, *Global Migration Perspectives*, 23, January.

Papadopoulou, A. (2005b), Regularization programmes: An effective instrument of migration policy?, Global Commission on International Migration, *Global Migration Perspectives*, 33, May.

Pastore, F. and Sciortino, G. (2003), *Italian Immigration Controls: Statistical Data (1991–2003)*, Cespi (Centro Studi di Politica Internazionale).

Pastore, F,. Monzini, P. and Sciortino, G. (2006), Schengen's soft underbelly? Irregular migration and human smuggling across land and sea borders to Italy, *International Migration*, 44, 95–119.

Patzwaldt, K. (2004), *Labour Migration in Eastern Europe and Central Asia: Current Issues and Next Political Steps*, UNESCO Series of Country Reports on the Ratification of the UN Convention on Migrants, 1 June.

Petrinioti, X. (1993), *Migration to Greece: A First Recording, Coding and Analysis*, Athens: Odysseas and Institute for International Relations (in Greek).

Pliez, O. (2003), *Villes du Sahara, urbanisation et urbanité dans le Fezzan libyen*, Paris, CNRS Editions, collection, Espaces et territoires.

Plummer, K. (2001), *Documents of Life 2: An Introduction to Critical Humanism*, London; Thousand Oaks, CA: Sage.

Salt, J. (2002), *Current Trends in International Migration in Europe*, Council of Europe, December.

Salt, J. and Stein, J. (1997), Migration as a business: The case of trafficking, *International Migration*, 35(4), 467–94.

Schuster, L. (2005a), *The Realities of a New Asylum Paradigm*, Centre on Migration Policy and Society, Working Paper No. 5, University of Oxford.

Schuster, L. (2005b). The continuing mobility of migrants in Italy: Shifting between places and status,' *Journal of Ethnic and Migration Studies*, 31(4), 757–74.

Shepherd, J. (2006), *Transnational Social Fields and the Experience of Transit Migrants in Istanbul*, Masters Thesis submitted to the University of Texas, May 2006.

Simon, J. (2006), Irregular transit migration in the Mediterranean: Facts, figures and insights, in: Sorensen, N. (ed.), *Mediterranean Transit Migration*, Copenhagen; Danish Institute for International Studies.

Sipavicieno, A. and Kanopiene, V. (1999), *Foreign Labour in Lithuania: Immigration, Employment and Illegal Work*, ILO/LUXEMBOURG Cooperation: Project RER/97/MO2/LUX.

Sitaropoulos, N. (2003), *Immigration Law and Management in Greece: Towards an Exodus from Underdevelopment and a Comprehensive Immigration Policy*, Athens: A. N. Sakkoulas Publishers.

Sitaropoulos, N. and Skordas, A. (2004), Why Greece is not a safe host country for refugees, *International Journal of Refugee Law*, 16(1), 25–52.

Skordas, A. (2002), The new immigration law in Greece: Modernization on the wrong track, *European Journal of Migration and Law*, 4, 23–48.

Sorensen, N. (2006), Mediterranean transit migration and development: Experience and policy options, in: Sorensen, N. (ed.), *Mediterranean Transit Migration*, Copenhagen: Danish Institute for International Studies.

Spener, D. (2001), Smuggling migrants through South Texas: Challenges posed by operation Rio Grande, in: Kyle, D., and Koslowski, R. (eds), *Global Human Smuggling: Comparative Perspectives*, Baltimore, MD: The Johns Hopkins University Press.

Szczepaniková, A. (2004), *The Power of a Refugee Camp: A view on a Czech 'Refugee Reality'*, online paper available at: www.migrationonline.cz

Thielemann, E. (2003) , Between interests and norms: Explaining burden-sharing in the European Union, *Journal of Refugee Studies*, 16(3), 253–73.

Triandafyllidou, A. (2000), 'Racists? Us? Are You Joking?' The Discourse of Social Exclusion of Immigrants in Greece and Italy, in King, R., Lazarides, G. and Tsardanidis, C. (eds), *Eldorado or Fortress? Migration in Southern Europe*, Basingstoke: Macmillan Press.

Triantafyllidou, A. and Gropas, R. (2006), Immigration to Greece: The case of Poles, Report prepared for the Research Project MIGSYS *Immigrants, policies and migration systems: An ethnographic comparative study*, Athens; Eliamep, July.

UNECE (1993), *International Migration Bulletin*, No. 3.

UNHCR (2006), *The Dublin Regulation; A UNHCR discussion paper*, Brussels: UNHCR.

UNHCR (2007a), *Asylum Levels and Trends in Industrialized Countries Second Quarter 2007: Statistical Overview of Asylum Applications Lodged in 31 European and 5 Non-European Countries*, Geneva: UNHCR.

UNHCR (2007b), *Response to the European Commission's Green Paper on the Future Common European Asylum System*, UNHCR Regional Representation, Brussels.

UNODC (2006), *Organized Crime and Irregular Migration from Africa to Europe*, United Nations Office on Drugs and Crime.

US Department of State (2006), *Country Report on Human Rights Practices 2006 – Algeria*, Bureau of Democracy, Human Rights, and Labour, 6 March.

Vaiou, D. and Hadjimichalis, K. (1997), *With the Sewing Machine in the Kitchen and the Poles in the Fields: Cities, Regions and Informal Labour*, Athens: Exantas (in Greek).

Van der Klaauw, J. (2007), Multi-dimensional migration challenges in North Africa, *Forced Migration Review*, 28, July.

Van Liempt, I. (2007), *Navigating Borders: Inside Perspectives on the Process of Human Smuggling into the Netherlands*, IMISCOE dissertations, Amsterdam: Amsterdam University Press.

Van Liempt, I. and Doomernik, J. (2006), Migrants agency in the smuggling process: The perspectives of smuggled migrants in the Netherlands, *International Migration*, 44(4), 165–90.

Van Selm, J. (ed.) (2000), *Kosovo's Refugees in the European Union*, London: Pinter.

Van Selm, J., Woroby, T., Patrick, E. and Matts, M. (2003), *Study on the Feasibility of Setting up Resettlement Schemes in EU Member States or at EU Level, against the Background of the Common European Asylum System and the Goal of a Common Asylum Procedure*, MPI on behalf of the European Commission, DG Justice and Home Affairs.

Van Selm, J. (2005a), *The Hague Program Reflects New European Realities*, Migration Information Source, MPI, Washington.

Van Selm, J. (2005b), *Georgia Looks West, But Faces Migration Challenges at Home*, Migration Information Source, Country Profile, MPI, Washington.

Van Selm, J. (2007), *Macedonia: At a Quiet Crossroads*, Migration Information Source, Country Profile, MPI, Washington.

Voronina, N. (2006), Outlook in migration policy reform in Russia: contemporary challenges and political paradoxes, in Rios, R. (ed.), *Planning and Managing Labour Migration*, Migration Perspectives Eastern Europe and Central Asia, IOM, October.

Voutira, E. (2003), Refugees: Whose term is it anyway? Emic and etic constructions of 'refugees' in Modern Greek, in van Selm, J., Kamanga, K., Morrison, J., Nadig, A., Vrzina, S. and van Willigen, L., *The Refugee Convention at fifty: A View from Forced Migration Studies*, Lanham, MD: Lexington Books.

Wahlbeck, O. (1998), Community work and exile politics: Kurdish refugee associations in London, *Journal of Refugee Studies*, 11(3), 215–30.

Wallace, C. and Stola, D. (eds) (2001), *Patterns of Migration in Central Europe*, Basingstoke: Palgrave Macmillan.
Wren, K. (2001), Cultural racism: Something rotten in the state of Denmark? *Social and Cultural Geography*, 2(2),141–62.
Yeganyan, G. (2006), The migration situation in Armenia: Challenges and solutions, in Rios, R. (ed.), *Planning and Managing Labour Migration*, Migration Perspectives Eastern Europe and Central Asia, IOM, October.
Zetter, R., Griffiths, D., Sigona, N., Hauser, M. (2002), *Survey on Policy and Practice Related to Refugee Integration: Summary Report*, Department of Planning, Oxford Brookes University, European Refugee Fund Community Actions, 2001/2.

Index